COGAT TRAINER
for Cognitive Abilities Test
Grade 7 & 8 (Level 13 & 14)

By Dustin Pack

Polemics Math

Polemics Math

Polemics Applications LLC produces educational books and apps for the iPhone, iPad and Android platforms. If you enjoy the content of this book feel free to look us up at www.polemicsmath.com. You'll find free content updated weekly and other materials to train in common core math and gifted & talented programs.

If you find a mistake we would love to fix it.
If you have comments or have trouble with a question
please send email to **info@polemicsmath.com**

This training guide has an iPhone and iPad Companion App! Train on the go with the Cognitive Ability Trainer:

http://bit.ly/Cogat7n8

Introduction

The struggle is what matters; this book is not just a practice test to toss at a child. It is a training guide. The language of all of our explanations, tips and tricks have a parental tone. To get maximum effect work through this book's sample tests and then review the answers together. Our appendices in the back not only tell you the answer but how to get to the answer. In all of these areas we are training the student's ability to think critically about each problem.

This book covers the nine categories of questions that your child will see on the middle school CogAT® tests. The material in this book is original in design and modeled after practice tests available online and from feedback from many forum discussions. In certain instances, we have increased the difficulty of the questions beyond the grade level of the student. The important lesson here is for the child to practice struggling with questions. The application of critical thinking in the face of uncertainty is a mainstay of all gifted and talented testing.

To test your student, simply take a sheet of scratch paper and have them mark the answers to each question. The answers to the questions are in the back of the book. As a bonus, for each visual type question we will redisplay the question and explain how you get to the correct answer. Good luck!

Be sure to check out Appendix F for some fun lessons on how to improve critical thinking.

Will this book be too easy for my 8th grader or too hard for my 7th grader? This book should be difficult for both grades to complete every answer correctly.

Our objectives for the student:

✓ Gain confidence through practice and review of each problem
✓ Learn how trick questions are made and how to beat them
✓ Increase critical thinking skills for lifelong use

Table of Contents

Each part of this book contains a full-length quiz on the subjects you'll find in the actual COGAT test. We have separated the sections into three broad categories: Visual Analysis, Language Skills and Numeric Skills. Each section has three different areas to test. At the end of each test is an answer key. We recommend you go through the tests writing answers on a piece of paper and then check your work with the answer key.

The appendices in this book are to help train you for certain material on the test. In appendix A-C we actually repeat every question found on the test and tell you how to get to the right answer. In Appendix D and E we will show you tips and tricks for the number type questions. Appendix F is a set of essays on how to think critically and achieve the best scores on the exam.

Visual Analysis

Visual Analysis

This book is best used as a training guide. When it comes to visual analysis and pattern recognition it is important to make distinctions on different levels. For example, is the pattern presented color based? Shape based? Or number based? Maybe a little of each?

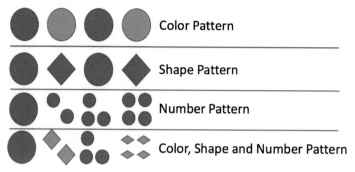

Color Pattern

Shape Pattern

Number Pattern

Color, Shape and Number Pattern

Sometimes shapes will rotate or turn in a question. This is an important clue to the right answer.

 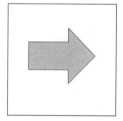  

Sometimes the pictures have a lot of **noise.** This is when there are parts of a picture that are just there to confuse you. In this sample what is consistent in each picture? It's the blue heart. All of those other shapes are there to mislead you. Sometimes everything in the picture is a clue to the answer and sometimes there are things there just to confuse you.

 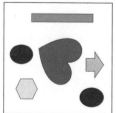 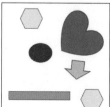 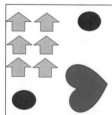

Visual Analysis: Figure Patterns

In figure pattern problems, you will look at three sample images and guess the correct image for the fourth panel. A pattern may be composed of two pictures such as the top left picture to the top right picture OR it may be a series of three pictures from top left to top right to bottom left. In some cases, the question shows you the pattern direction using arrows (see Question 1) and in some cases you need to guess the direction. Patterns will only go in one of those two ways.

Figure Pattern: Question 1

(A)   (B)   (C)   (D)

(A)   (B)   (C)   (D)

Figure Pattern: Question 3

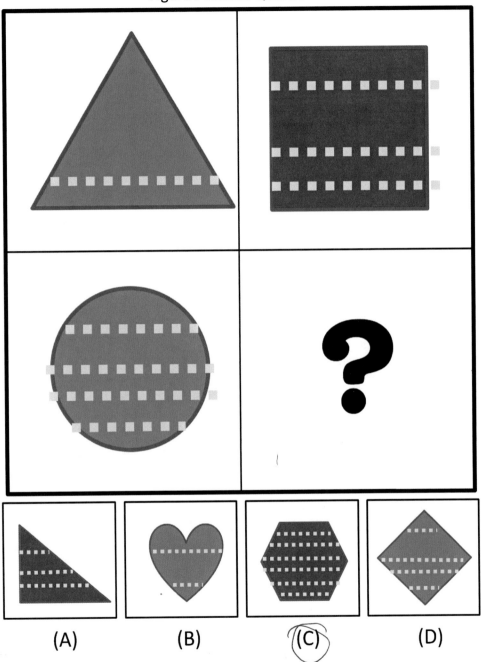

(A) (B) (C) (D)

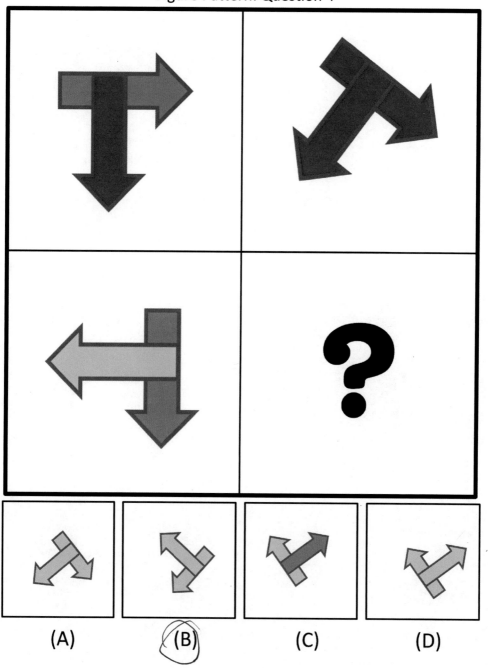

(A)   (B)   (C)   (D)

Figure Pattern: Question 5

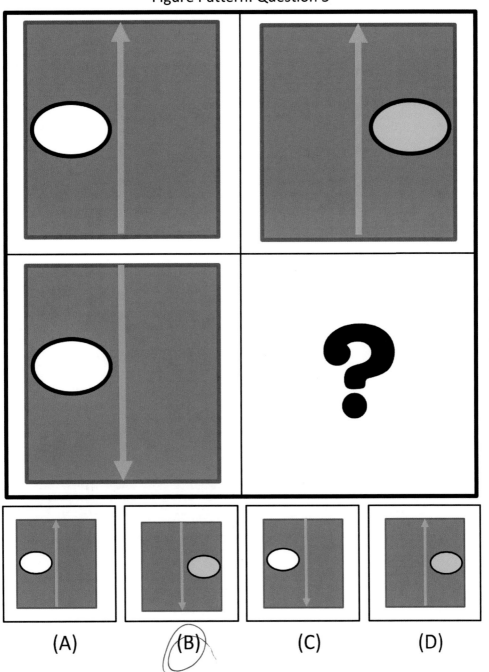

(A)   (B)   (C)   (D)

Figure Pattern: Question 6

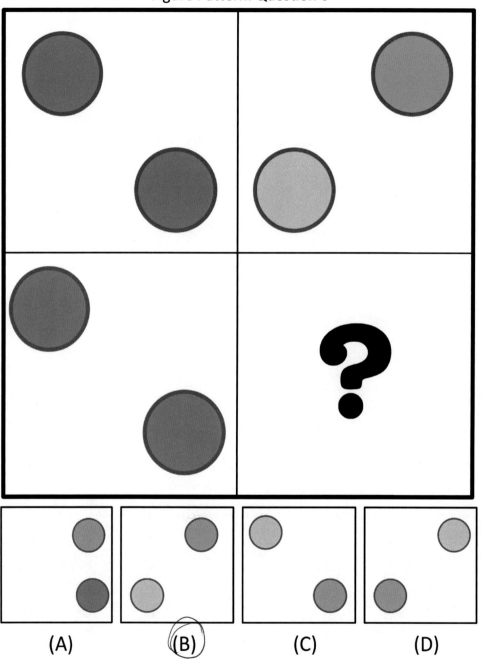

(A)   (B)   (C)   (D)

Figure Pattern: Question 7

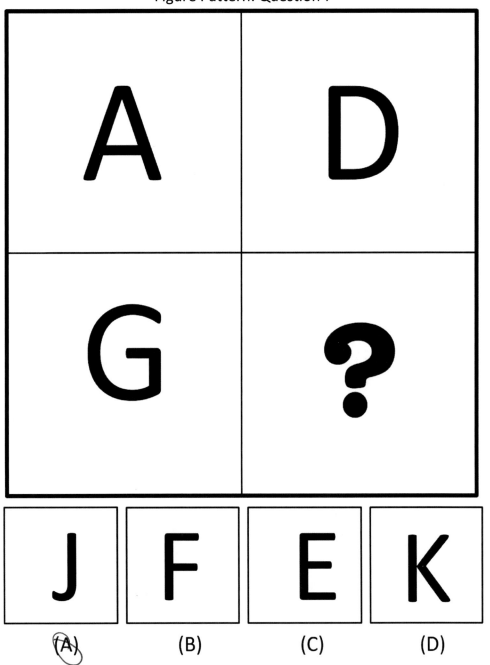

Figure Pattern: Question 8

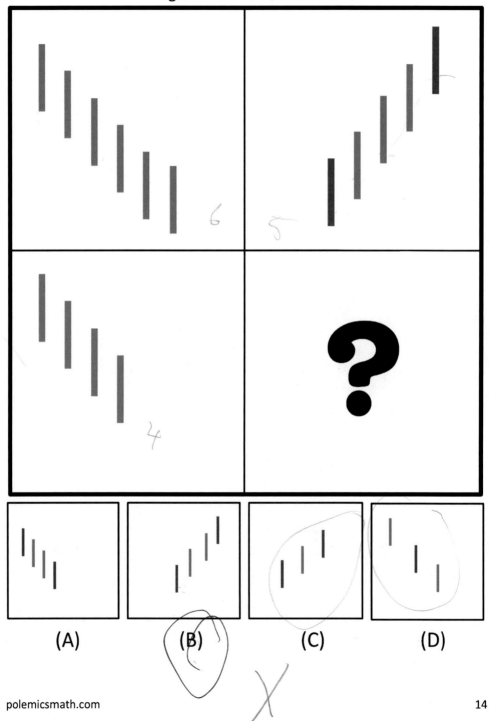

(A) (B) (C) (D)

Figure Pattern: Question 9

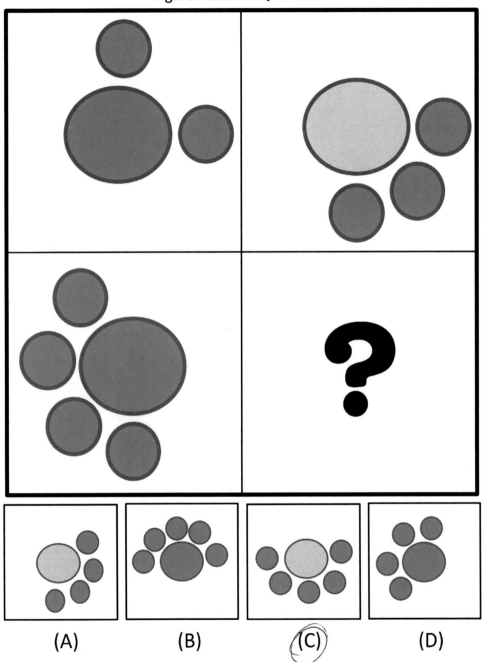

(A) (B) (C) (D)

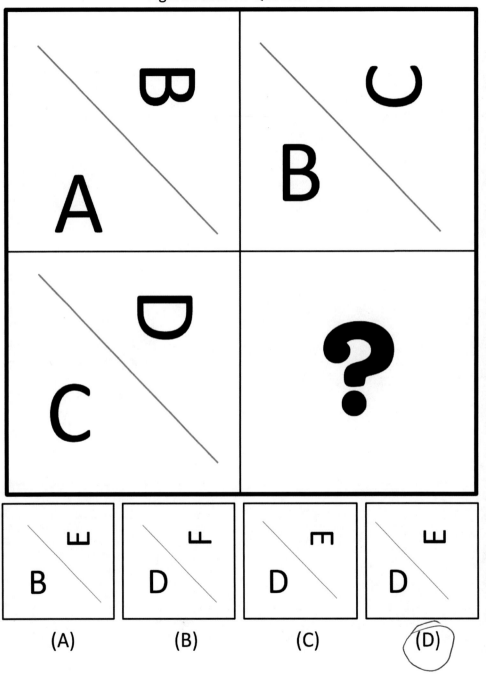

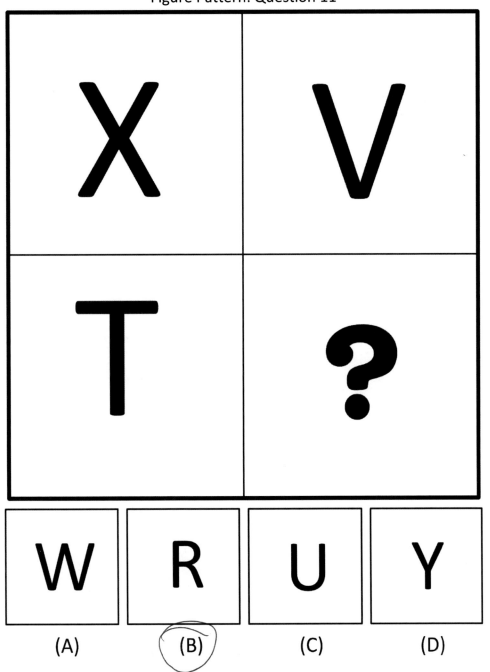

(A) W   (B) R   (C) U   (D) Y

Figure Pattern: Question 12

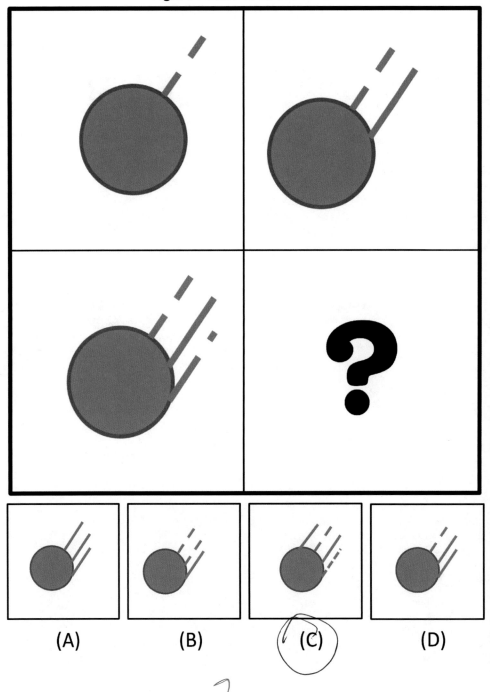

(A)   (B)   (C)   (D)

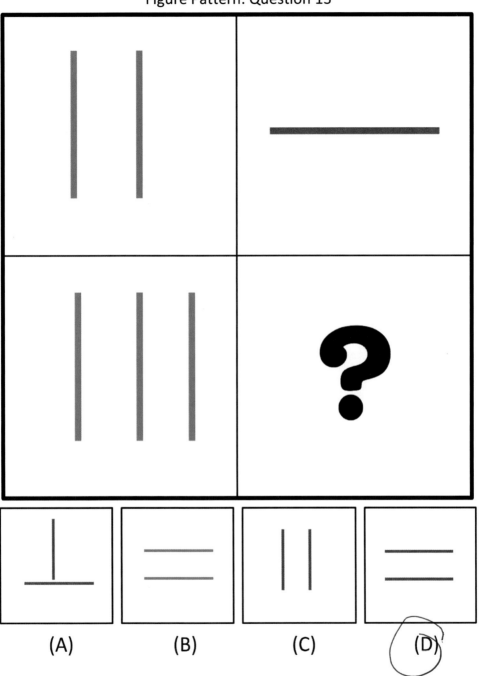

(A)   (B)   (C)   (D)

Figure Pattern: Question 14

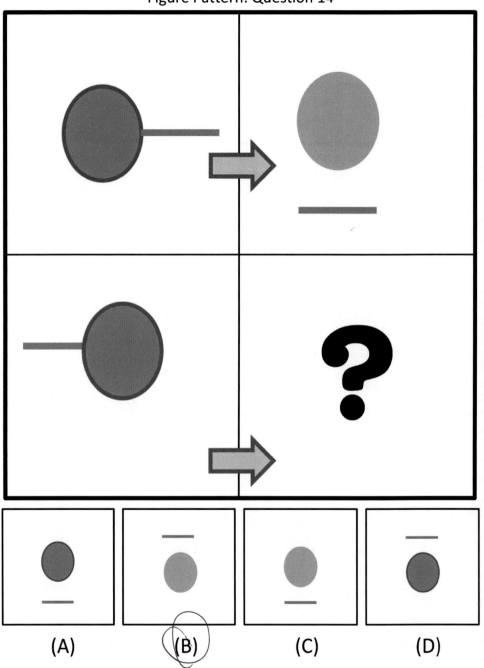

(A) (B) (C) (D)

Figure Pattern: Question 15

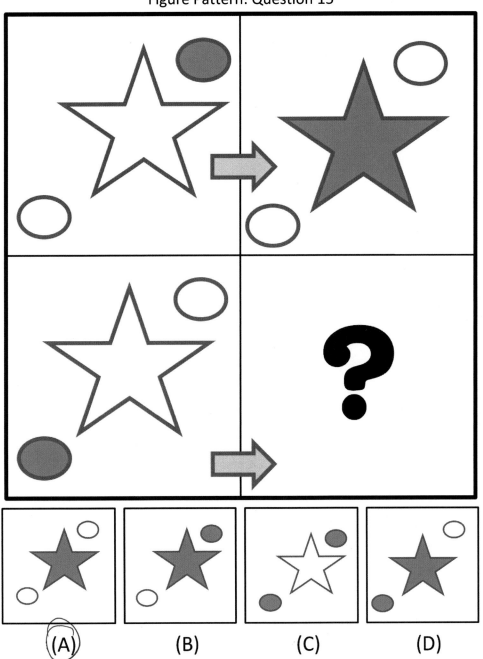

(A)   (B)   (C)   (D)

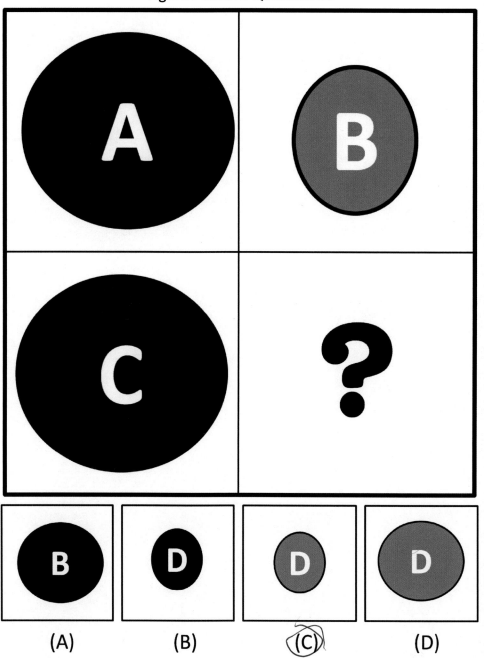

(A)   (B)   (C)   (D)

Figure Pattern: Question 17

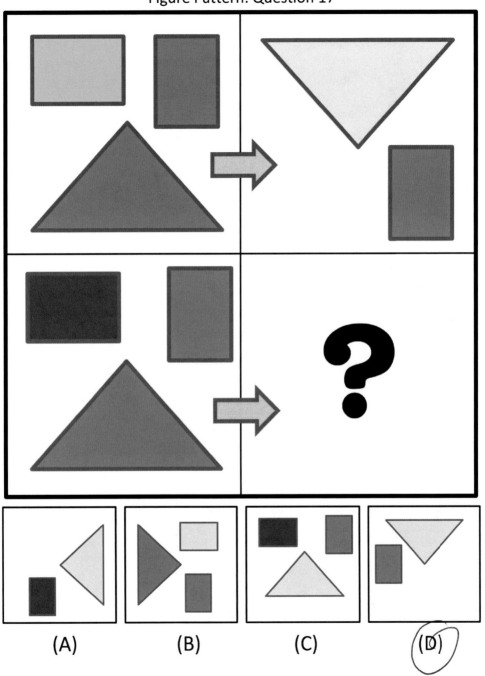

(A) (B) (C) (D)

Figure Pattern: Question 18

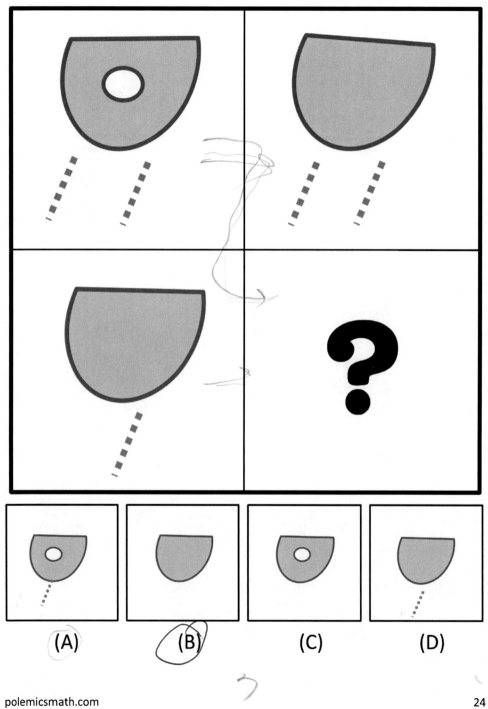

(A) (B) (C) (D)

Figure Pattern: Question 19

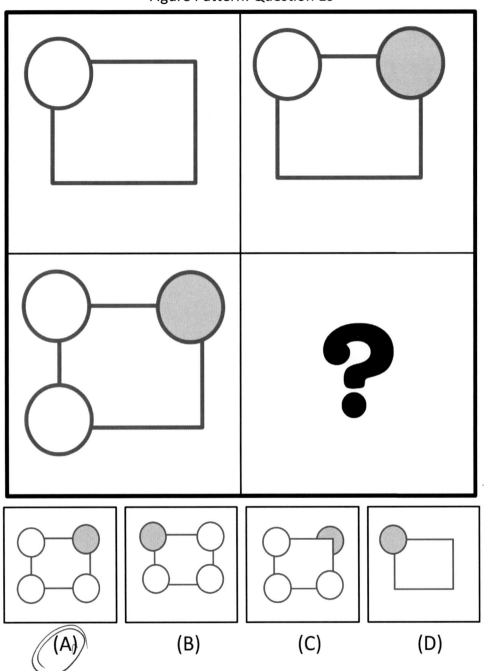

(A)   (B)   (C)   (D)

Figure Pattern: Question 20

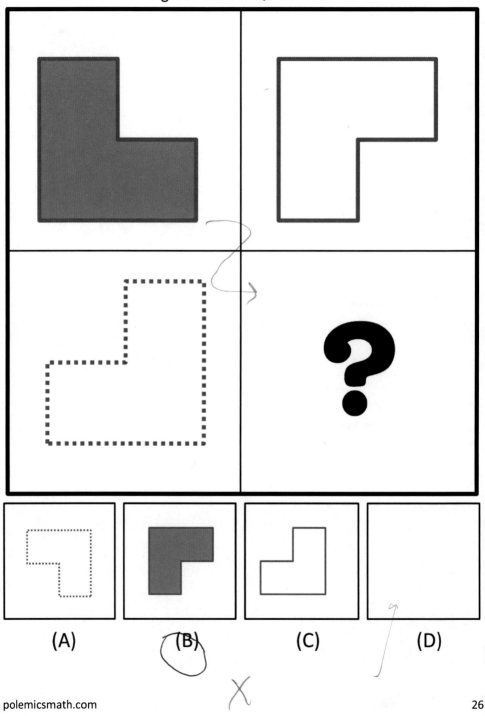

(A)   (B)   (C)   (D)

Figure Pattern: Question 21

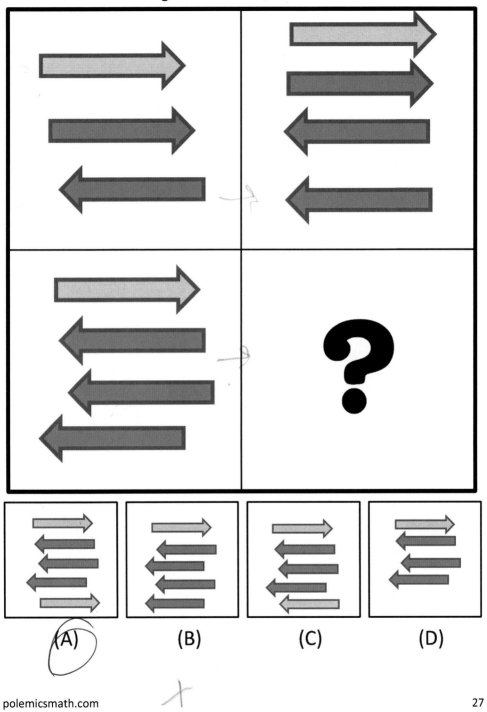

(A)   (B)   (C)   (D)

Figure Pattern: Question 22

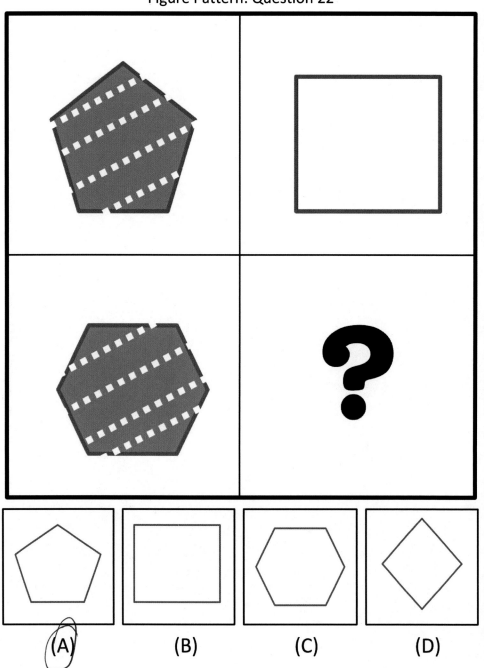

(A)   (B)   (C)   (D)

Figure Pattern: Question 23

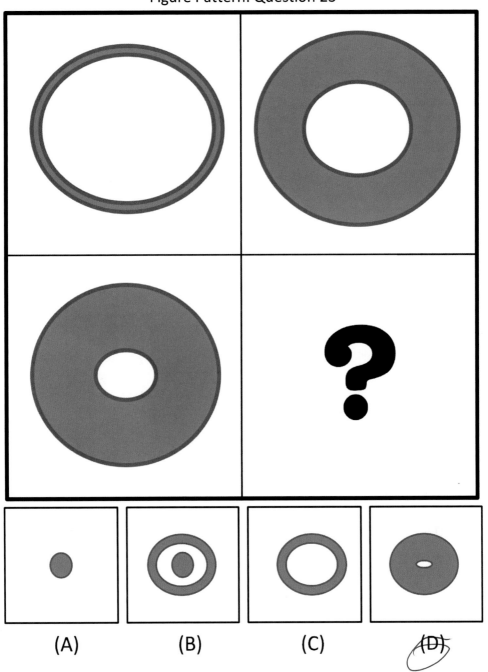

(A) (B) (C) (D)

Figure Pattern: Question 24

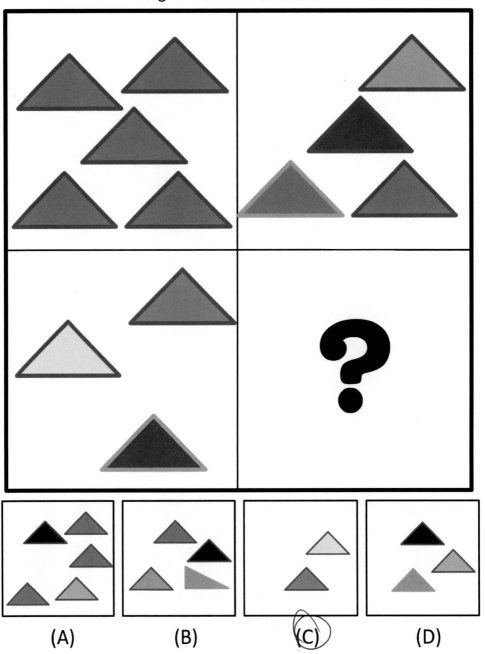

(A) (B) (C) (D)

Figure Pattern: Question 25

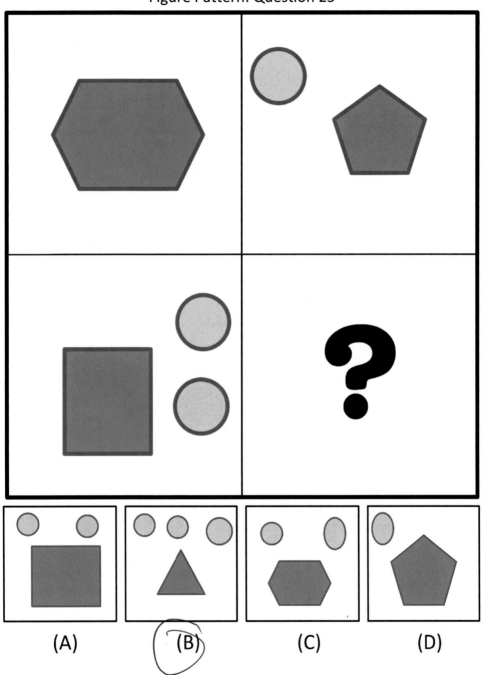

(A) (B) (C) (D)

Figure Pattern: Answer Key

Question	Answer	Question	Answer
1	D	14	B
2	D	15	A
3	C	16	C
4	B	17	D
5	B	18	B
6	B	19	A
7	A	20	D
8	C	21	B
9	C	22	A
10	D	23	D
11	B	24	C
12	C	25	B
13	D		

Please See Appendix A for a detailed explanation for each of these answers. Appendix A is written for adults to explain to the student how a piece of critical thinking occurred on a problem. Tip: use this review time as a discussion platform on other ways the child may have found the answers.

Visual Analysis: Figure Matrices

The figures in each pattern follow a pattern much like the previous section. The pattern reads from left to right and top to bottom. Pick the next picture to complete the pattern. Ask yourself these questions:

- Do the shapes change size?
- Do the number of shapes go up or down?
- Do the colors of the shapes change?
- Are the shapes on top of each other or separated?
- Did the shapes rotate?
- How many sides does each shape have in the pattern?

Any one or more of these questions can assist you in finding the pattern.

In the below example the top left white box rotates to the left AND changes colors to orange. When looking at this problem we can ask "what happened to the white box?" Then we can say "The white box rotated and changed colors to orange" Next, we can look at the blue triangle and ask, "What will the blue triangle look like when it rotates and changes color to orange?" The answer is (D). Now practice this thought process on the questions in this section.

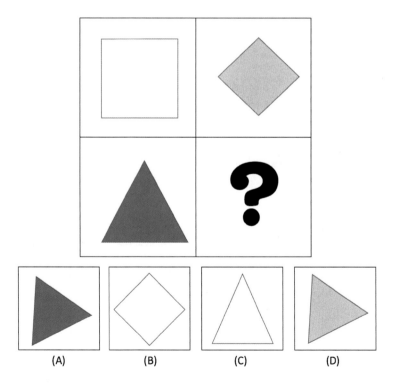

Figure Matrices: Question 1

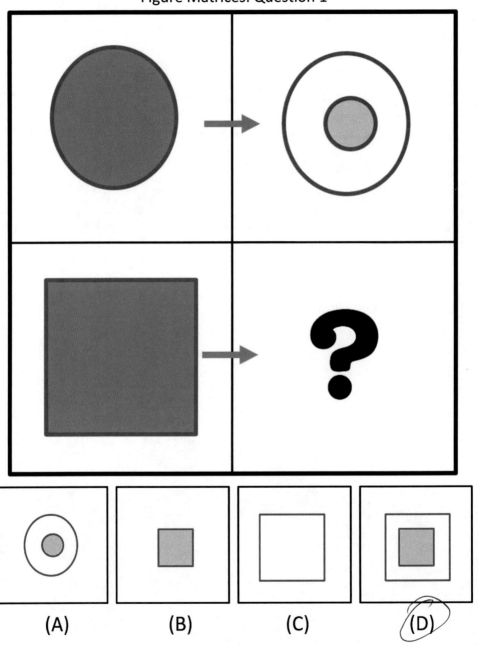

(A)   (B)   (C)   (D)

Figure Matrices: Question 2

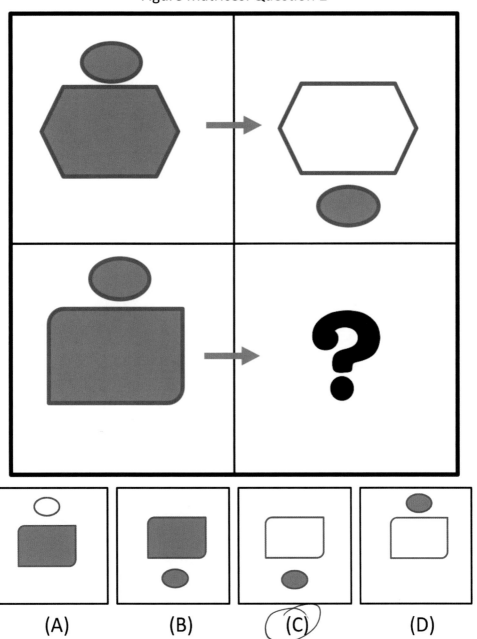

(A)   (B)   (C)   (D)

Figure Matrices: Question 3

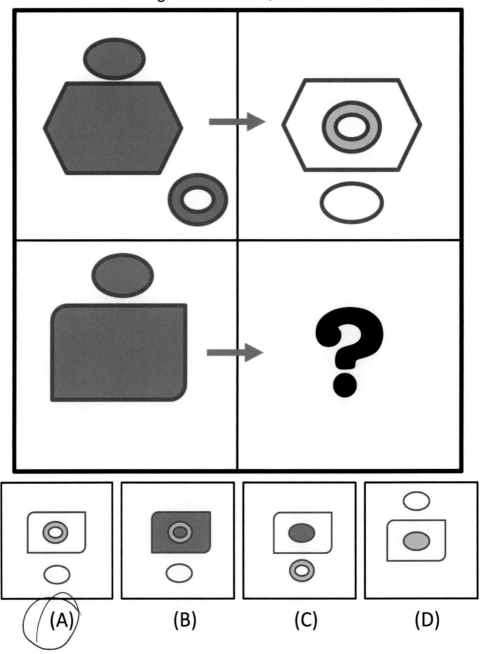

(A)   (B)   (C)   (D)

Figure Matrices: Question 4

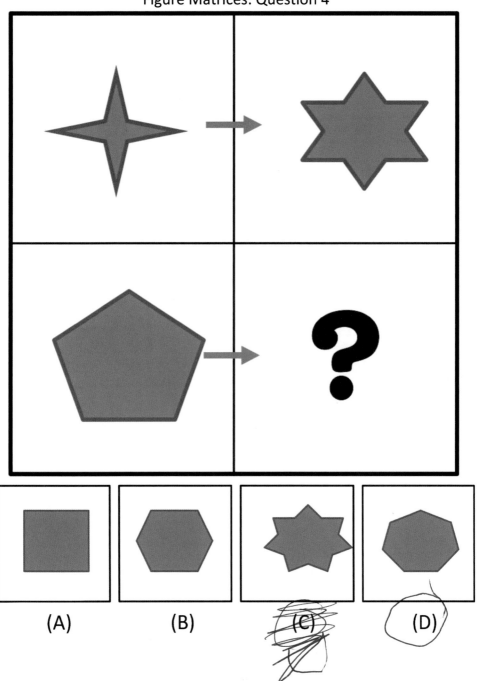

(A)   (B)   (C)   (D)

Figure Matrices: Question 5

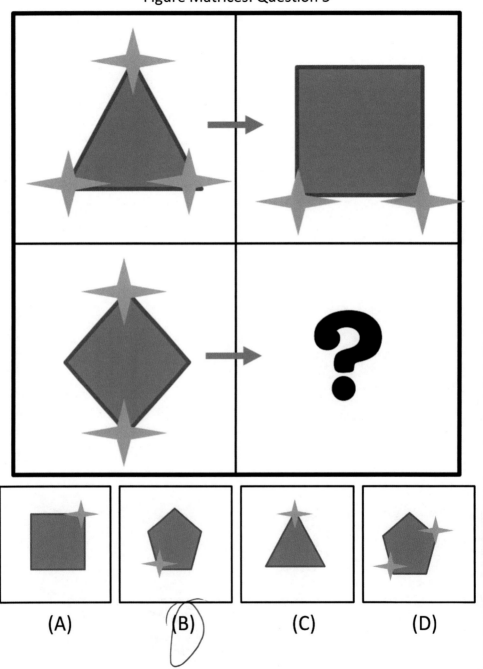

(A)   (B)   (C)   (D)

Figure Matrices: Question 6

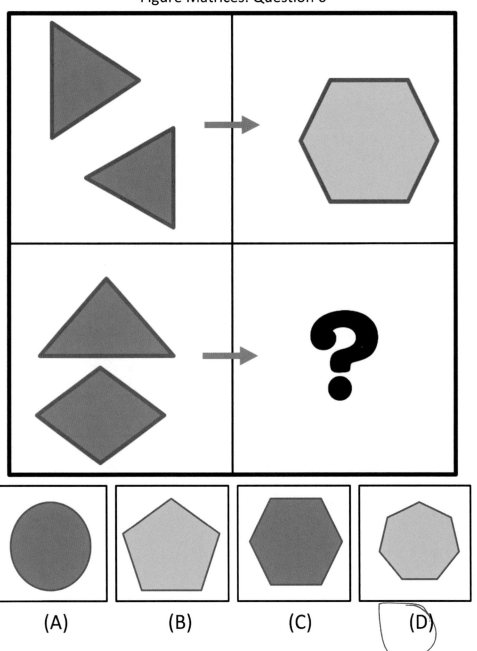

(A)   (B)   (C)   (D)

Figure Matrices: Question 7

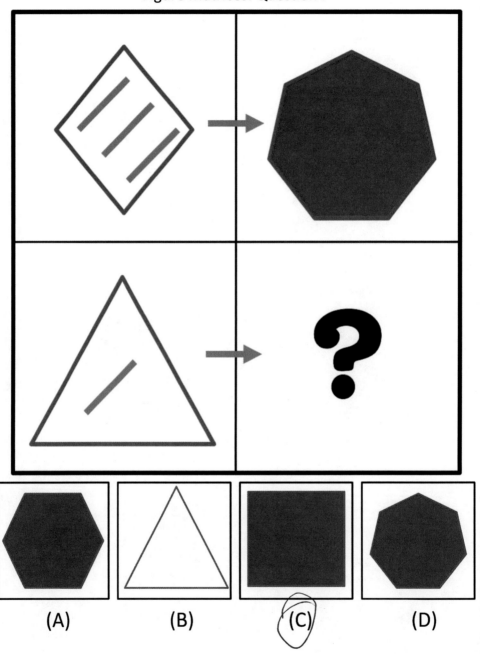

(A)   (B)   (C)   (D)

Figure Matrices: Question 8

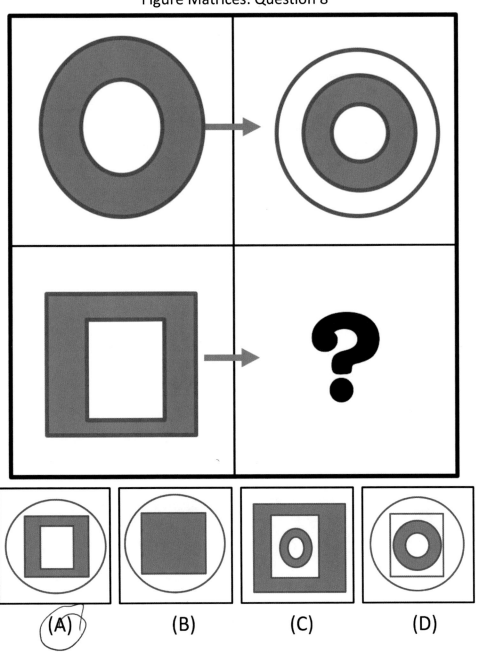

(A)   (B)   (C)   (D)

Figure Matrices: Question 9

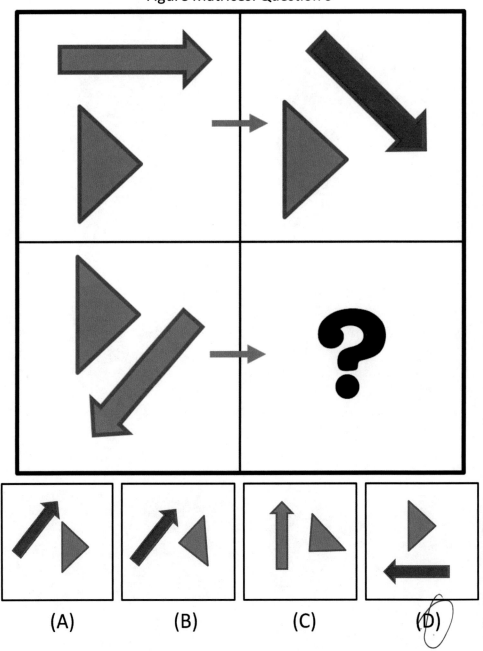

(A)   (B)   (C)   (D)

Figure Matrices: Question 10

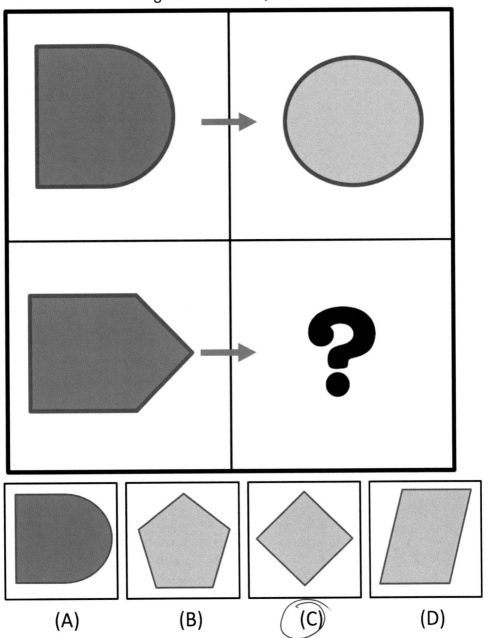

(A)   (B)   (C)   (D)

Figure Matrices: Question 11

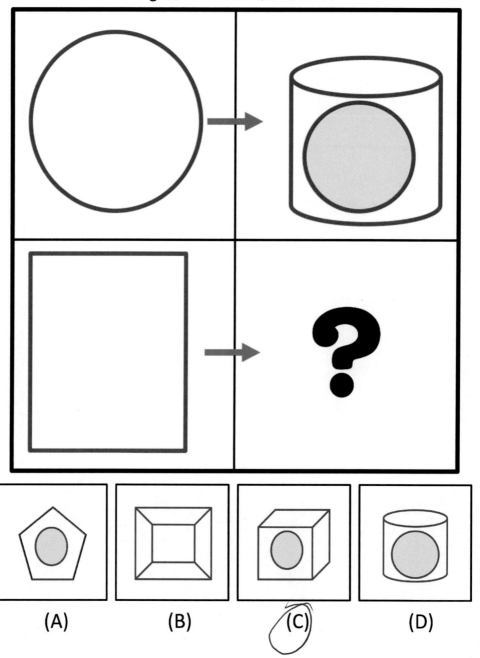

(A)   (B)   (C)   (D)

Figure Matrices: Question 12

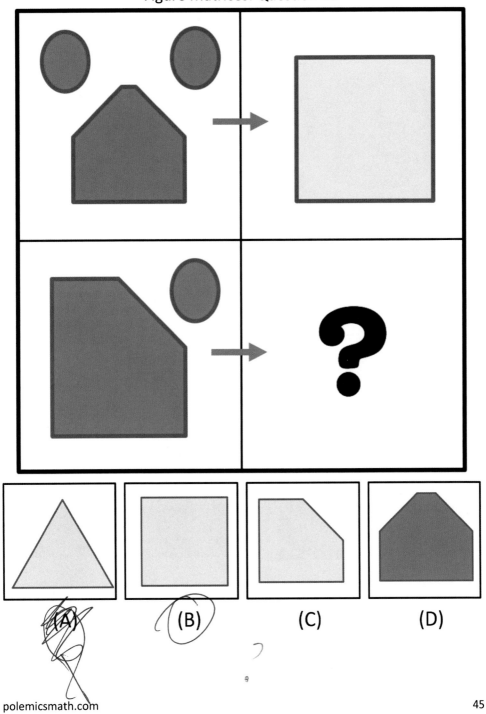

(A) (B) (C) (D)

Figure Matrices: Question 13

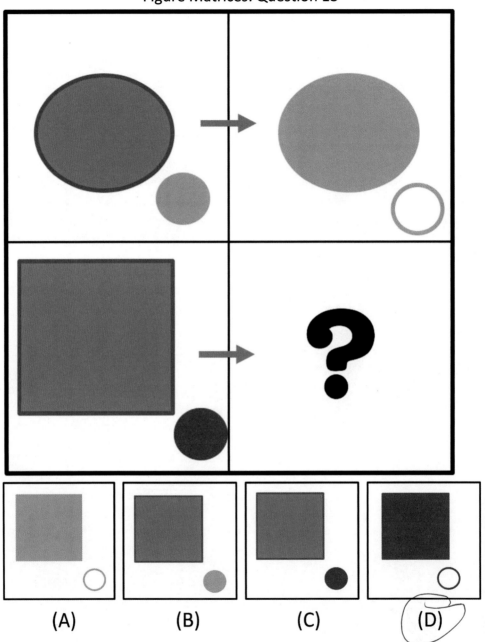

(A)   (B)   (C)   (D)

Figure Matrices: Question 14

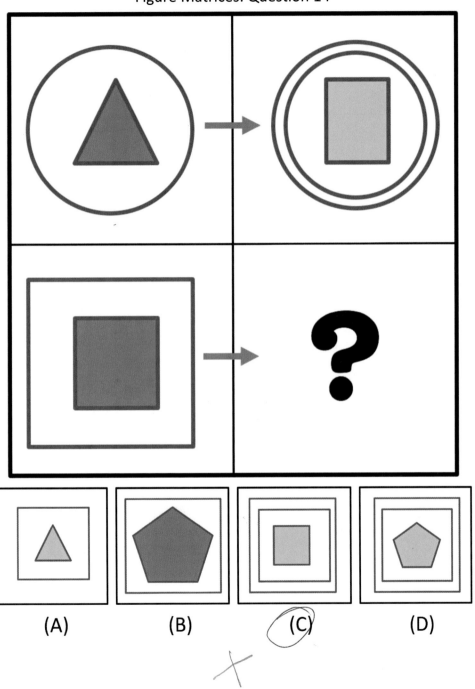

(A)   (B)   (C)   (D)

Figure Matrices: Question 15

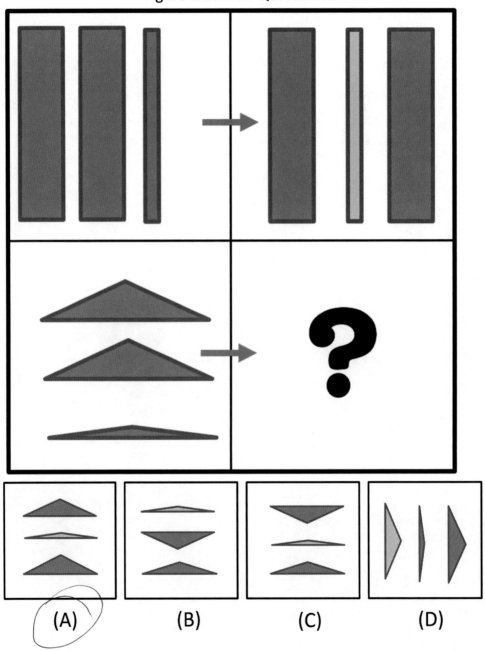

(A)   (B)   (C)   (D)

Figure Matrices: Question 16

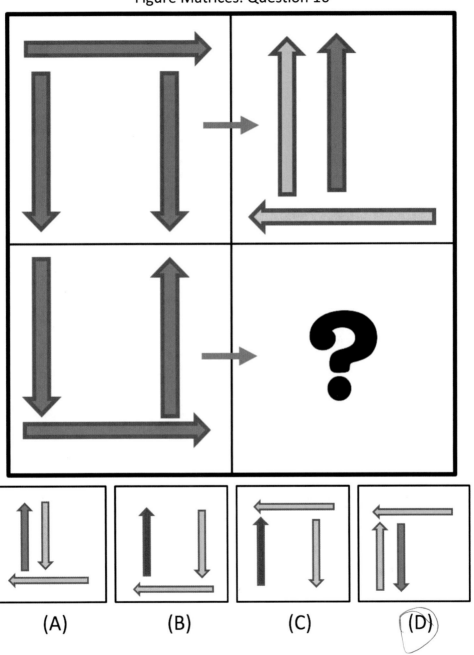

(A)   (B)   (C)   (D)

Figure Matrices: Question 17

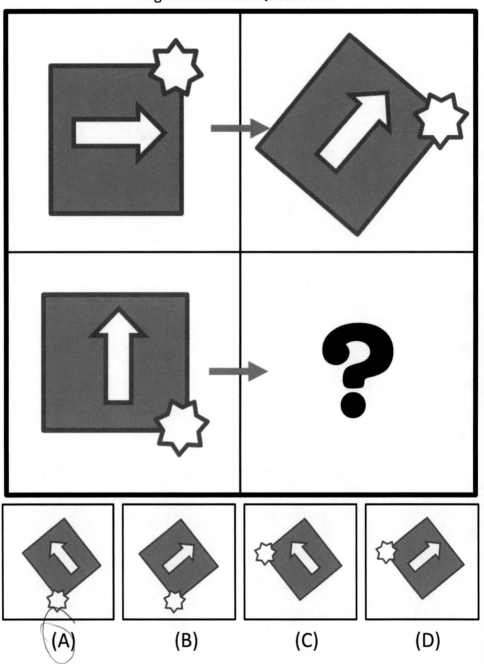

(A) (B) (C) (D)

Figure Matrices: Question 18

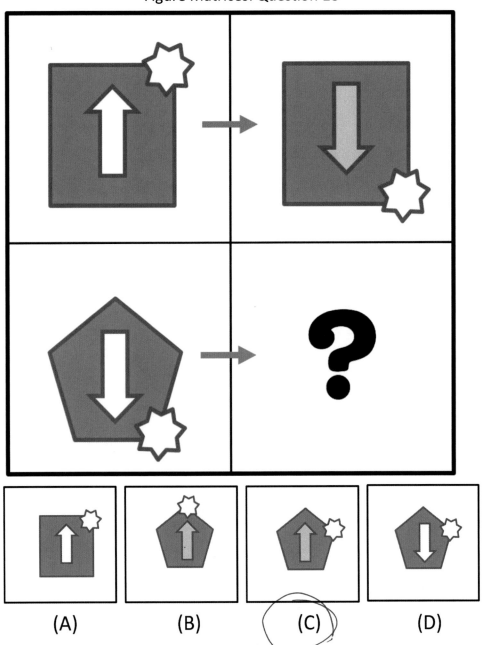

(A) (B) (C) (D)

Figure Matrices: Question 19

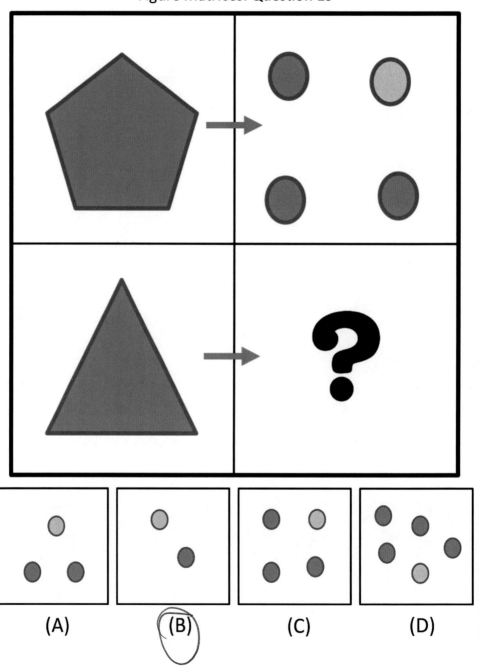

(A)   (B)   (C)   (D)

Figure Matrices: Question 20

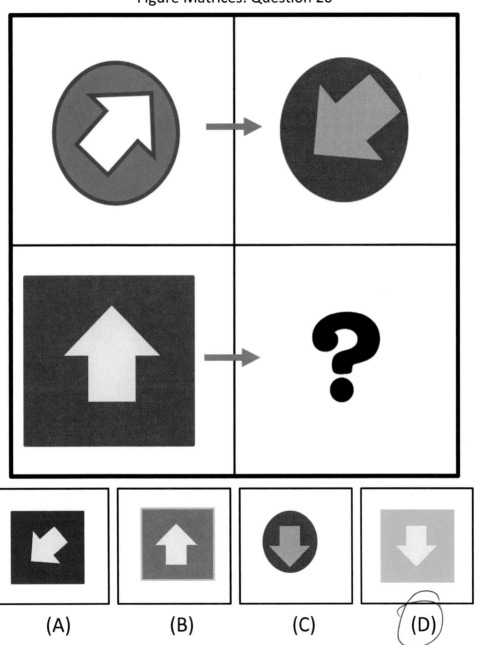

(A)   (B)   (C)   (D)

Figure Matrices: Question 21

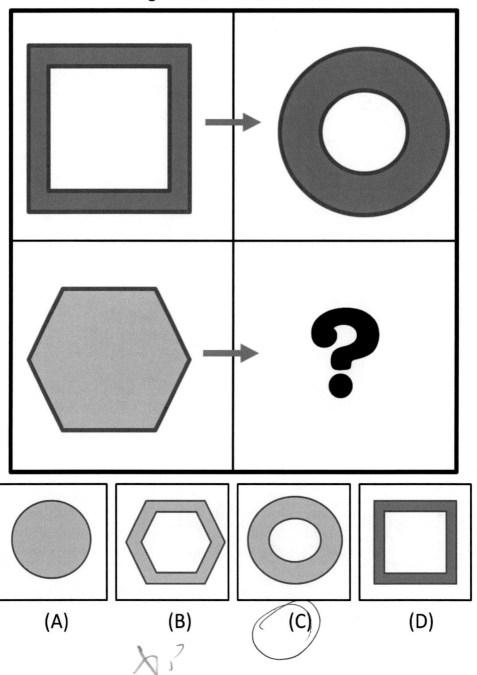

(A) (B) (C) (D)

Figure Matrices: Question 22

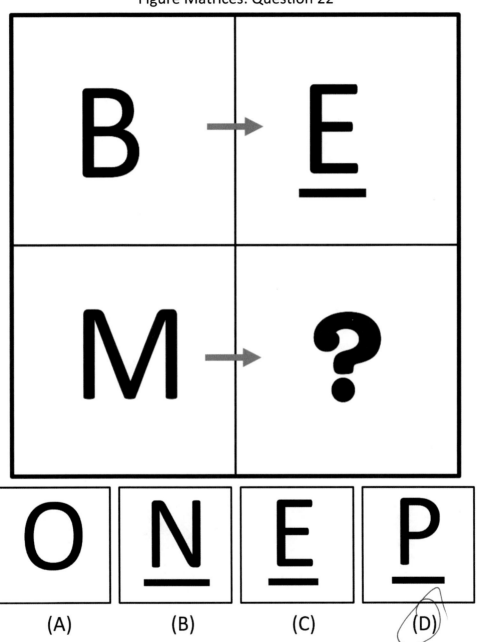

(A)   (B)   (C)   (D)

Figure Matrices: Question 23

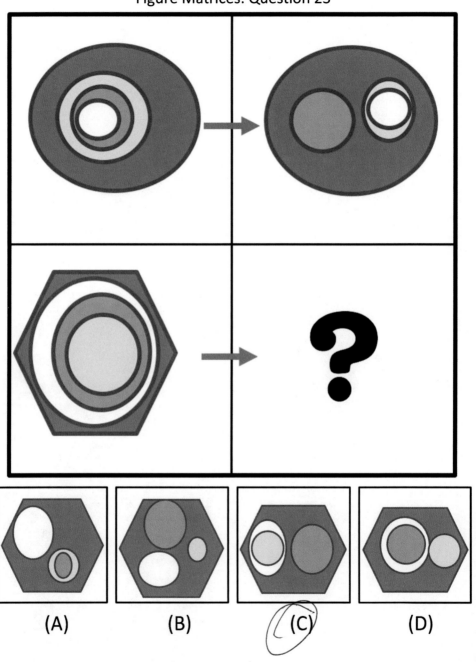

(A)   (B)   (C)   (D)

Figure Matrices: Question 24

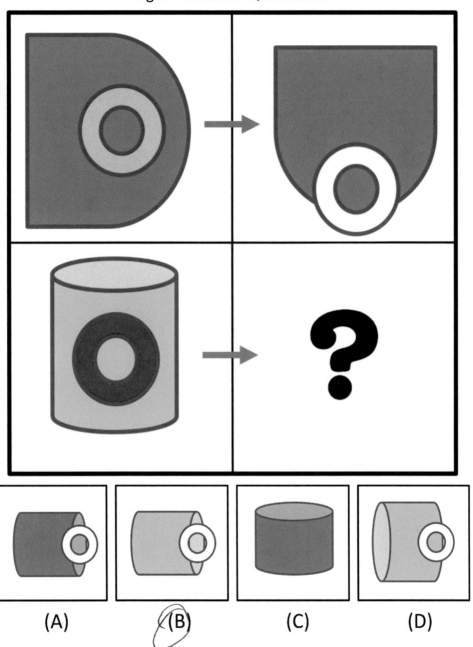

(A)   (B)   (C)   (D)

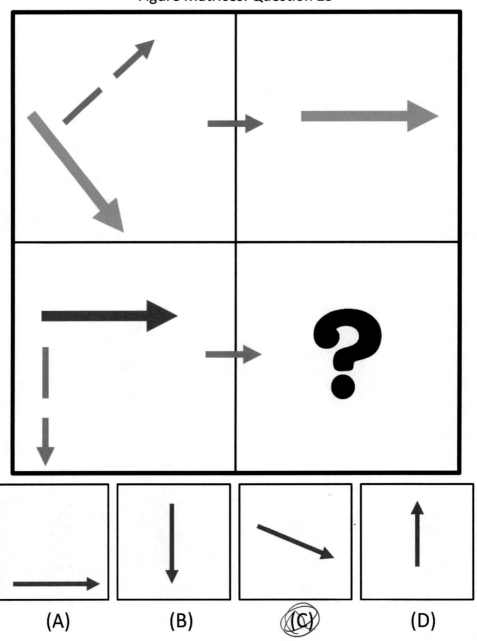

(A)   (B)   (C)   (D)

Figure Matrices: Answer Key

Question	Answer	Question	Answer
1	D	14	D
2	C	15	A
3	A	16	D
4	D	17	A
5	B	18	C
6	D	19	B
7	C	20	D
8	A	21	A
9	D	22	D
10	C	23	C
11	C	24	B
12	B	25	C
13	D		

Please See Appendix B for a detailed explanation for each of these answers.
Note: Questions 20-25 were from a different (but similar) Gifted and Talented
Test Trainer, congrats if you answered all of them correctly!

Visual Analysis: Paper Folding

Paper folding is a practice of visualizing symmetry. Each question shows a piece of paper that is folded and cut. The answers all show what the paper will look like when it was unfolded. You can make a quick demonstration of this by folding a piece of paper in half, cutting a half heart shape out and then showing how it looks when unfolded.

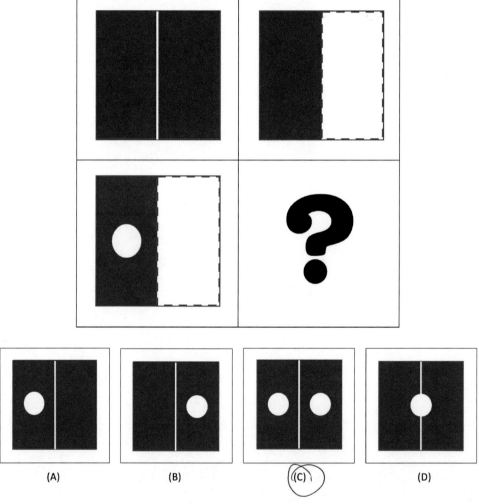

(A)   (B)   ((C))   (D)

Let's do the first one together. Here the paper is folded in half along the white line, then a hole is punched. Which answer shows what the paper looks like unfolded? Answer C is correct; it shows two holes punched in the proper (symmetrical) locations.

Paper Folding: Question 1

(A)   (B)   (C)   (D)

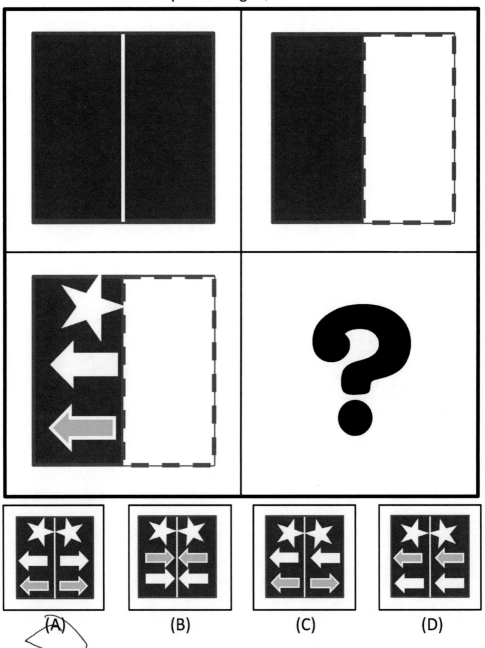

(A) (B) (C) (D)

Paper Folding: Question 3

(A)   (B)   (C)   (D)

Paper Folding: Question 4

(A) (B) (C) (D)

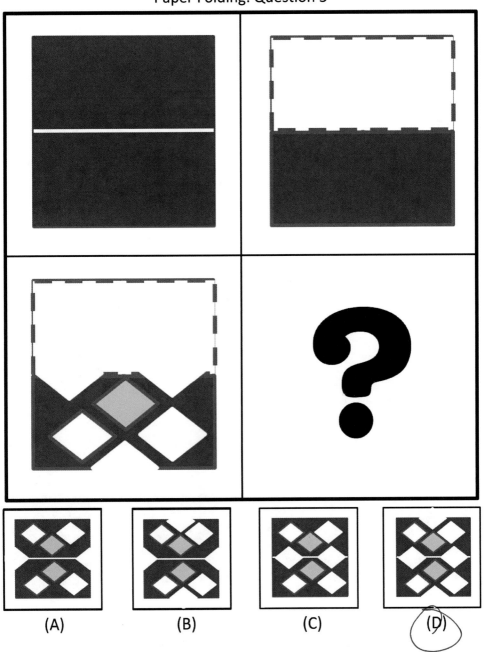

(A)   (B)   (C)   (D)

Paper Folding: Question 6

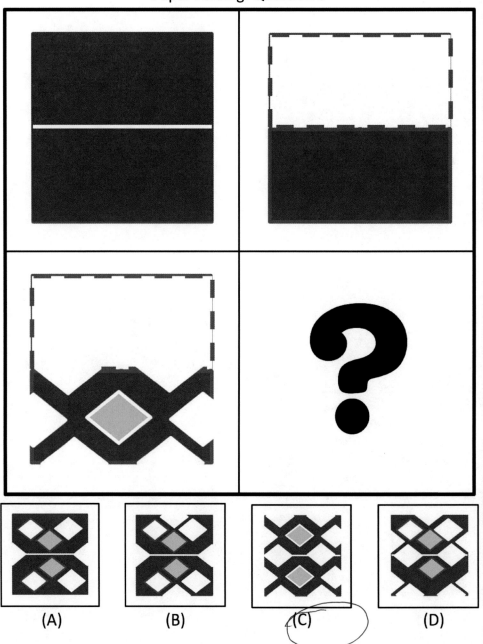

(A) (B) (C) (D)

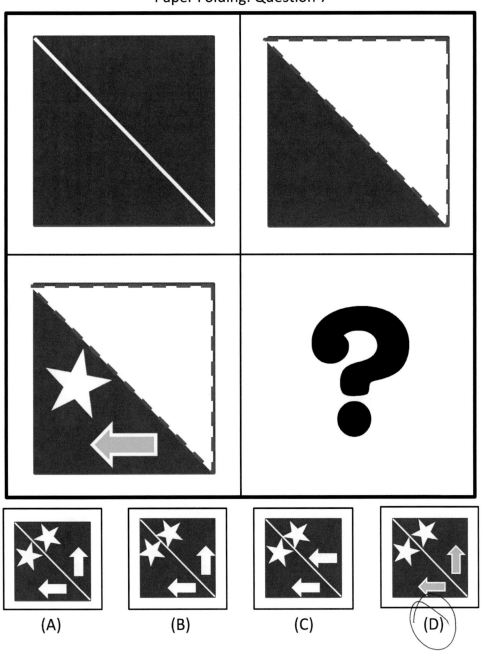

(A)   (B)   (C)   (D)

Paper Folding: Question 8

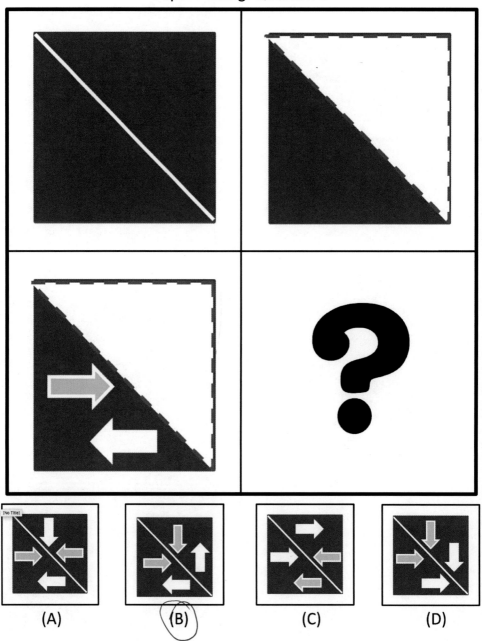

(A) (B) (C) (D)

Paper Folding: Question 9

(A) (B) (C) (D)

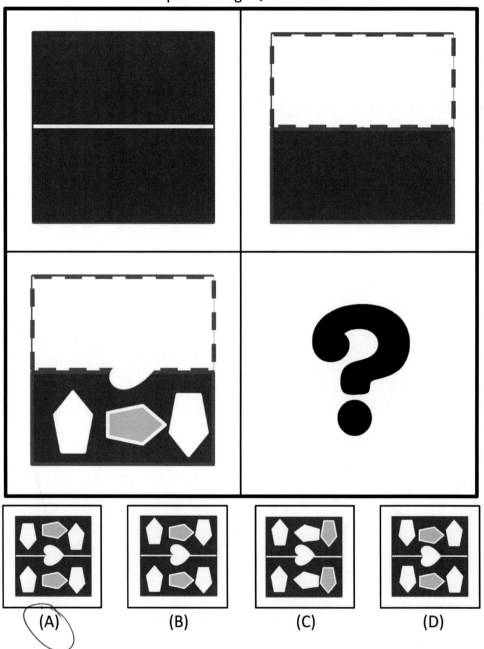

Paper Folding: Question 11

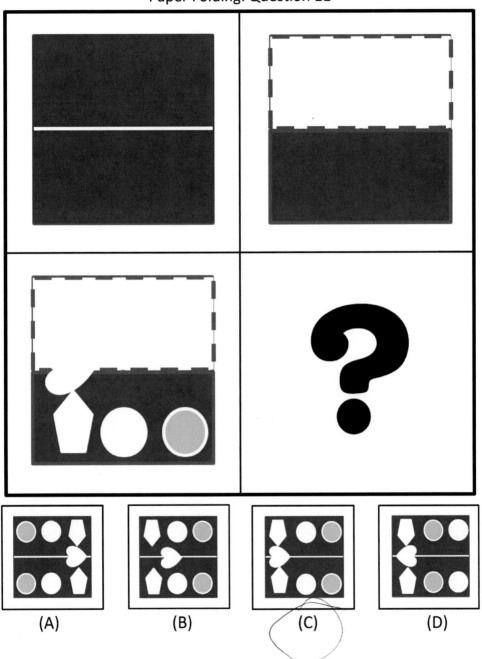

(A) (B) (C) (D)

Paper Folding: Question 12

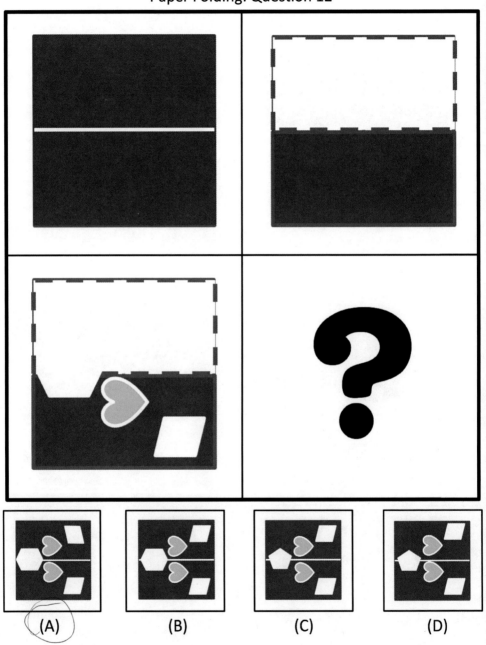

Paper Folding: Question 13

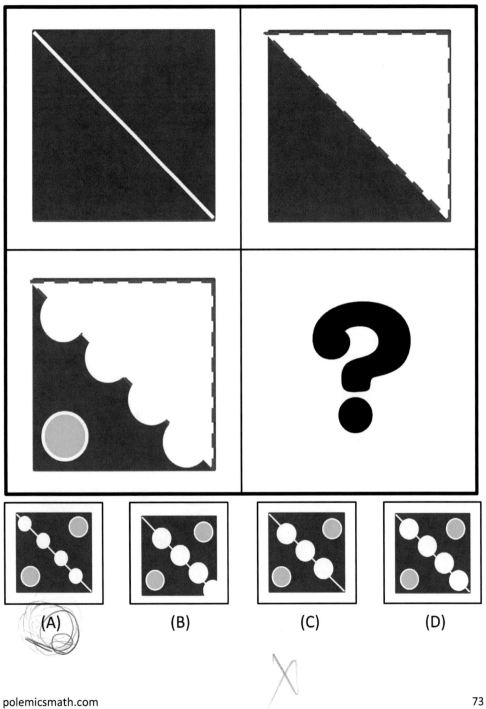

(A)　(B)　(C)　(D)

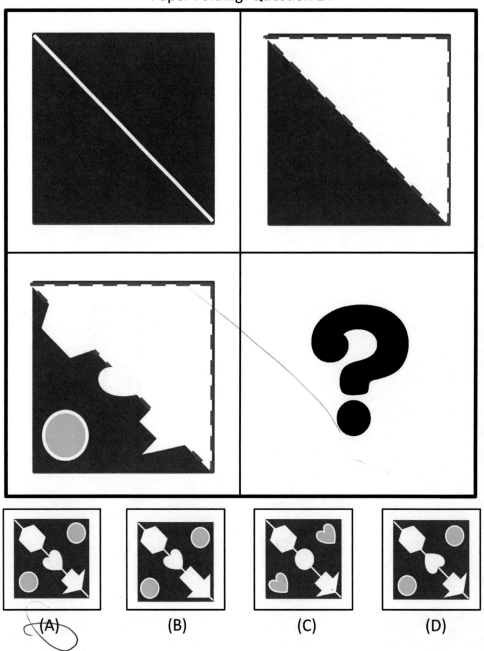

(A)   (B)   (C)   (D)

Paper Folding: Question 15

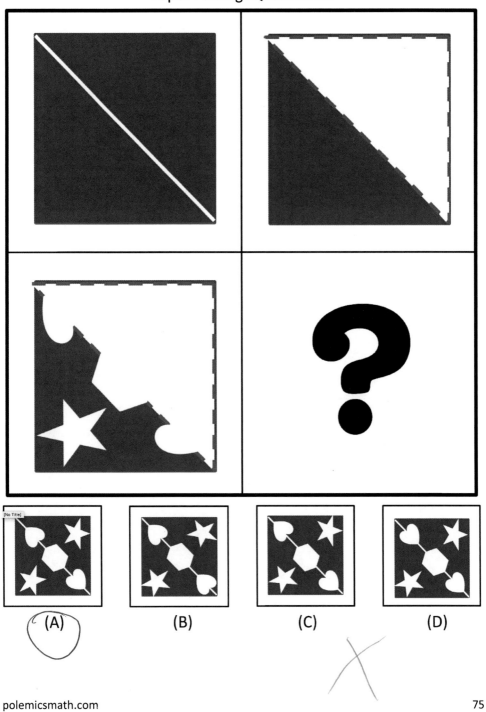

(A)   (B)   (C)   (D)

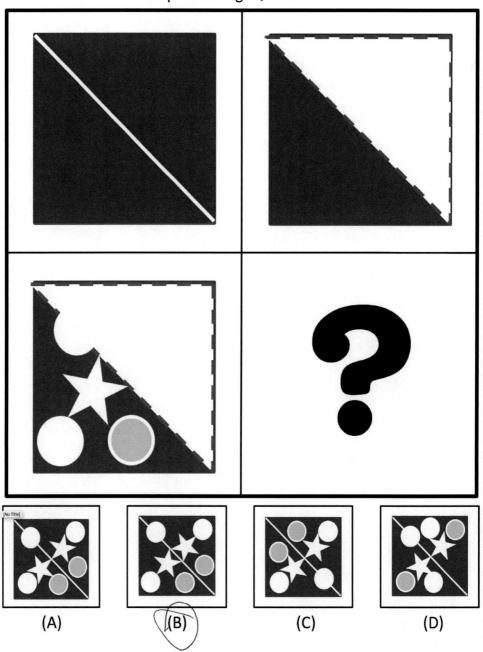

(A)　　　　(B)　　　　(C)　　　　(D)

Paper Folding: Answer Key

Question	Answer
1	C
2	A
3	C
4	B
5	D
6	C
7	D
8	B
9	D
10	A
11	C
12	A
13	D
14	A
15	C
16	B

Please See Appendix C for a detailed explanation for each of these answers.

Numeric Skills

Numeric Skills: Number Series

Each of these number series show a particular pattern. Pick the number that is the next number in the series. Tip: patterns may be made by adding, subtracting, multiplying or dividing by a certain number.

1. 243   81   27   9   ?
    a) 9   b) 1   c) 3   d) 6   e) 2

2. 21   7   24   8   36   ?
    a) 9   b) 16   c) 15   d) 19   e) 12

3. 3   5   8   12   ?
    a) 17   b) 14   c) 35   d) 36   e) 13

4. 0   1   1   2   3   5   8   ?
    a) 12   b) 22   c) 15   d) 26   e) 13

5. 17   13   11   7   ?
    a) 5   b) 4   c) 9   d) 2   e) 10

6. 33   25   16   9   ?

   a) 9   b) 0   c) 4   d) 10   e) 1

7. 216   125   64   27   ?

   a) 4   b) 15   c) 5   d) 8   e) 14

8. 4   9   16   25   ?

   a) 33   b) 59   c) 48   d) 40   e) 29

9. 1   5   12   22   35   51   ?

   a) 130   b) 73   c) 76   d) 70   e) 67

10. 0   1   1   2   3   5   8   ?

   a) 12   b) 9   c) 19   d) 10   e) 13

11.   **12   16   21   27   ?**
    a) 70   b) 49   c) 59   d) 66   e) 34

12.   **14   42   15   45   ?**
    a) 23   b) 12   c) 16   d) 22   e) 24

13.   **2   3   5   7   11   13   ?**
    a) 22   b) 17   c) 28   d) 23   e) 15

14.   **1   3   9   27   ?**
    a) 81   b) 150   c) 125   d) 78   e) 114

15.   **2   6   13   23   36   52   ?**
    a) 68   b) 71   c) 117   d) 73   e) 86

16.   **0**   **1**   **4**   **9**   **16**   **25**   **?**

   a) 36   b) 37   c) 43   d) 50   e) 32

17.   **14**   **18**   **23**   **29**   **?**

   a) 44   b) 54   c) 67   d) 36   e) 57

18.   **12**   **16**   **21**   **27**   **?**

   a) 44   b) 41   c) 34   d) 46   e) 48

19.   **6**   **3**   **7**   **4**   **8**   **?**

   a) 5   b) 4   c) 8   d) 2   e) 7

20   **3**   **6**   **12**   **24**   **?**

   a) 48   b) 45   c) 50   d) 44   e) 47

21. 7 11 18 28 ?

   a) 34   b) 37   c) 41   d) 45   e) 42

22. 1 10 17 22 25 ?

   a) 26   b) 27   c) 20   d) 23   e) 29

23. 1 2 3 3 2 ?

   a) 2   b) 0   c) 6   d) 1   e) 4

24. 12 24 36 48 ?

   a) 59   b) 52   c) 74   d) 60   e) 66

25. 160 150 141 133 ?

   a) 125   b) 129   c) 132   d) 124   e) 126

Number Series: Answer Key

Question	Answer	Question	Answer
1	C	14	A
2	E	15	B
3	A	16	A
4	E	17	D
5	A	18	C
6	C	19	A
7	D	20	A
8	A	21	C
9	D	22	A
10	E	23	D
11	E	24	D
12	C	25	E
13	B		

Please See Appendix D for a detailed explanation on how to find these answers and **additional practice**.

Numeric Skills: Number Equations

This is, for many, the very hardest part of the test. You'll take the numbers and the operator symbols [+ - / x ()] in each question and make an equation that, when solved will equal one of the answers presented.

Example: Given **1 1 +** make an equation that will solve to one of these numbers (1, 2, 3, 4, 5). The test taker would move the 1 1 and + to form an equation such as 1 + 1 and see if 1 + 1 equals one of the answers presented.

This one can be very frustrating so do take your time with each. We have an appendix at the end that explains all of the answers to these questions.

1. **6 8 1 1 2 + + + / ()**
    a) 10   b) -4   c) 8   d) 11   e) 16

2. **3 9 15 - x ()**
    a) -16   b) 30   c) 31   d) 13   e) 12

3. **15 5 2 10 - - + ()**
    a) -18   b) 15   c) 14   d) 13   e) 18

4. **5 4 6 - x**
    a) 16   b) -20   c) 15   d) 19   e) 18

5. **3 27 2 () / -**
    a) 7   b) 5   c) 29   d) 14   e) 30

6. <u>2 5 1 2 / + x</u>

   a) 5.5   b) 4.5   c) 8   d) 7   e) 5

7. <u>16 4 2 - / ()</u>

   a) 7   b) -4   c) 15   d) 14   e) 6

8. <u>9 3 -3 + x ()</u>

   a) 15   b) 12   c) 18   d) 9   e) 17

9. <u>1 2 2 3 + + x</u>

   a) 6   b) 9   c) 7   d) -7   e) 15

10. <u>3 8 2 + /</u>

   a) 8   b) 6   c) 9   d) 5   e) 7

11. <u>6 3 2 + x</u>

    a) 21   b) 12   c) 13   d) 14   e) 11

12. <u>21 4 3 + / ()</u>

    a) 3   b) 4   c) 12   d) 32   e) 33

13. <u>2 2 3 5 x + + ()</u>

    a) 15   b) 30   c) 31   d) 25   e) 20

14. <u>4 6 3 2 () () / / +</u>

    a) 3   b) 4   c) 17   d) 18   e) 15

15. <u>24 2 1 x - ()</u>

    a) 45   b) 47   c) 51   d) 46   e) 48

Number Equations: Answer Key

Question	Answer
1	C
2	E
3	E
4	D
5	A
6	B
7	E
8	C
9	B
10	E
11	B
12	A
13	A
14	B
15	B

Please See Appendix E for a detailed explanation for how to find each of these answers.

Numeric Skills: Number Inequalities

This section asks you to "solve" A and B and then determine if the answer of A is > < or = the answer to B. So each problem here is like 3 different problems that must all be solved correctly to win the overall problem.

1. **A.** **Diameter / 2**
    B. **Radius x 2**
    a) A > B   b) A < B   c) A = B

2. **A.** **15% of 30**
    B. **1/2 + 3 + 1/2**
    a) A > B   b) A < B   c) A = B

3. **A.** **Fifty six cents**
    B. **A dollar and eleven cents / 2**
    a) A > B   b) A < B   c) A = B

4. **A.** **15% of 10**
    B. **10% of 15**
    a) A > B   b) A < B   c) A = B

5. **A.** **1/5 x 1/5**
    B. **1/5 + 1/5**
    a) A > B   b) A < B   c) A = B

6.   **A.**   **2 ^ 6**

        B.   **193.5 / 3**

a) A > B   b) A < B   c) A = B

7.   **A.**   **98 x (1/2)**

        B.   **100 x (4/3)**

a) A > B   b) A < B   c) A = B

8.   **A.**   **Square root of 64**

        B.   **6**

a) A > B   b) A < B   c) A = B

9.   **A.**   **4 quarts**

        B.   **1 gallon**

a) A > B   b) A < B   c) A = B

10.   **A.**   **80 x 15 / 5**

        B.   **(15 / 5) x 80 x 1**

a) A > B   b) A < B   c) A = B

11.   **A.**   **75 x (1/2)**

          B.   **100 x (4/3)**

          a) A > B   b) A < B   c) A = B

12.   **A.**   **6 / 5**

          B.   **3 / 6**

          a) A > B   b) A < B   c) A = B

13.   **A.**   **30 x 15 / 5**

          B.   **30 x (15 / 5)**

          a) A > B   b) A < B   c) A = B

14.   **A.**   **Chance to roll a 1 on a 6 sided die**

          B.   **Chance to roll a 5 on a 6 sided die**

          a) A > B   b) A < B   c) A = B

15.   **A.**   **43 / 2**

          B.   **63.5 / 3**

          a) A > B   b) A < B   c) A = B

16.   **A.**   **66 x 3**
          B.   **340 / 3**
          a) A > B   b) A < B   c) A = B

17.   **A.**   **1 liter**
          B.   **1 quart**
          a) A > B   b) A < B   c) A = B

18.   **A.**   **Sides on a rectangle**
          B.   **Sides on a pentagram**
          a) A > B   b) A < B   c) A = B

19.   **A.**   **1 yard**
          B.   **1 meter**
          a) A > B   b) A < B   c) A = B

20   **A.**   **Oranges at half price**
          B.   **Oranges at a quarter price**
          a) A > B   b) A < B   c) A = B

21.   **A.**   **Sum of two #s where each > 0**

         B.   **A positive # X a negative #**

         a) A > B   b) A < B   c) A = B

22.   **A.**   **3 ^ 3**

         B.   **6 ^ 2**

         a) A > B   b) A < B   c) A = B

23.   **A.**   **Sides on a triangle**

         B.   **Sides on a hexagon**

         a) A > B   b) A < B   c) A = B

24.   **A.**   **0.25 x 2**

         B.   **(1/2) + (1/4)**

         a) A > B   b) A < B   c) A = B

25.   **A.**   **1 / Y**

         B.   **Y (Where Y > 1)**

         a) A > B   b) A < B   c) A = B

Number Inequalities: Answer Key

Question	Answer
1	B
2	A
3	A
4	C
5	B
6	B
7	B
8	A
9	C
10	C
11	B
12	A
13	C

Question	Answer
14	C
15	A
16	A
17	A
18	B
19	B
20	A
21	A
22	B
23	B
24	B
25	B

There is no detailed explanation for this section. In general, review the answers missed with the test taker. This section more than any other is testing your general knowledge of math operations such as fractions, multiplication and the ability to understand numbers from words.

Language Skills

Language Skills: Sentence Completion

This section is a standard fill in the blank type of response. Read the question and look for clues as to what the right word is. This isn't just a test of how large your vocabulary is, it can also be about finding a clue and making an educated guess of the right answer.

1. **The water was put through several filters to get it to _____ .**
   In the end it was cleaned of all impurities.
   a) trap   b) clarify   c) surpass   d) swelter

2. **The two wrestlers locked arms and began to _____ with one**
   another pushing and pulling to gain advantage in the match.
   a) grunt   b) shackle   c) glut   d) grapple

3. **Always trust the advice of a good hotdog _____ ; they have**
   sampled the whole menu and are experts in the subject.
   a) barter   b) sage   c) conveyor   d) connoisseur

4. **The car was considered a _____ vehicle because it ran on**
   both gas and electricity.
   a) ethanol   b) SUV   c) green   d) hybrid

5. **To get to the under side of the engine we had to _____**
   the outer parts of of the hood and cover assembly.
   a) install   b) repair   c) dismantle   d) assemble

6. The old wolf looked _____ standing there in the snow. Its fur was matted with dirt and its head hung low from walking across the plains for several days.

   a) capacious   b) audacious   c) haggard   d) benign

7. To remark in a way that is short and expressive is said to be _____ .

   a) fallacy   b) arrogant   c) pity   d) pithy

8. We think the tax policy will have a(n) _____ effect. It will neither help nor hurt the treasury or the working class.

   a) fastidious   b) benign   c) bland   d) bizarre

9. Sometimes you have to use different words to _____ what you mean. Words have meaning and in science you need to be precise.

   a) articulate   b) exemplify   c) augment   d) attribute

10. The people of the coast were considered _____. They moved from place to place in search of their next meal.

    a) saintly   b) great   c) diplomatic   d) nomadic

11. She was very _____, always preferring to go with the flow and never really getting excited when things didn't go as planned.

a) loath   b) casual   c) arrogant   d) excited

12. The friar demanded that the weary group of travelers _____ their pagan ways by giving up their traditions in favor of the new religion.

a) exemplify   b) facilitate   c) renounce   d) evolve

13. The public announcement of his running for election was a(n) _____ grab for power over the political council. His actions are as clear to anyone now as ever.

a) overt   b) profound   c) gullible   d) arrogant

14. The student body took a vote on which bus would be taken on the band trip. Everyone _____ that the blue bus was best.

a) concurred   b) congested   c) compromised d) consulted

15. There was a warning on the label that said "Do not _____ with the safety seal or the device may break."

a) tamper   b) taper   c) twist   d) tap

16. When two friends disagree on something they will usually
_____ and find a solution that is acceptable to both of
them rather than to continue fighting over it.
a) clamber   c) concur   c) contest   d) compromise

17. The _____ of the evil wizard was that he could save the lives
of others but could not save his own life.
a) tragedy   b) tonic   c) contest   d) cipher

18. A Soldier will shine her boots and polish the buttons on her
dress uniform to _____ pride, duty and discipline in herself
and her unit.
a) instill   b) install   c) reject   d) shackle

19. The guide could speak French but this particular _____ used in
West Africa had confused him, causing us to wait for a friend who
knew the local language.
a) dialect   b) cipher   c) diametric   d) decipher

20. Swamp water was thick with plants and dirt particles. I looked to
the edge trying to see the bottom but it was too _____.
a) murky   b) clear   c) frigid   d) thin

End Of Section!
Keep Up The Good Work!

Sentence Completion: Answer Key

Question	Answer	Question	Answer
1	B	11	B
2	D	12	C
3	D	13	A
4	D	14	A
5	C	15	A
6	C	16	D
7	D	17	A
8	B	18	A
9	A	19	A
10	D	20	A

There is no detailed explanation for this section. Review the answers missed with the test taker. Tips:

- Review each answer in a question and try to force yourself to pick from the top two answers. This will help make sure you have considered each question thoroughly.
- The elimination method works for this section just as you did for the visual problems in previous sections.
- As with all language sections, having a strong vocabulary is key to winning.

Language Skills: Verbal Classification

Questions in this section will show you three words that are related in a certain way. Pick a word from the set of answers that are also related in that same certain way. To say it another way, you will be classifying the words. Maybe they are items in a kitchen, things that you do or types of food. When you figure out the classification, choose a word from the answers that most closely fits that classification.

1. **math**   **reading**   **science**   _e_
    a) physics   b) college   c) homework
  X d) grades   e) diploma

2. **action**   **drama**   **horror**   _d_
    a) philosophy   b) comedy   c) fear
  ✓ d) fiction   e) cartoon

3. **debug**   **test**   **code**   _a_
  X a) archive   b) execute   c) update
    d) monitor   e) design

4. **rosemary**   **mint**   **dill**   _E_
  X a) potato   b) cilantro   c) tomato
    d) sugar   e) pepper

5. **hockey**   **basketball**   **baseball**   _a_
    a) soccer   b) player   c) coach
    d) goal   e) stick

6. **broil**   **grill**   **fry**   *a*
    ✗ a) cook   b) melt   c) prepare
       d) bake   e) package

7. **smartphone**   **television**   **computer**   *A*
       a) laptop   b) DVD   c) VCR
       d) camera   e) mouse

8. **diplomat**   **soldier**   **senator**   *C*
       a) secretary   b) tour guide   c) judge
       d) programmer   e) doctor

9. **Bush**   **Clinton**   **Reagan**   *C*
       a) America   b) men   c) president
       d) congress   e) Washington

10. **eggs**   **bacon**   **cereal**   *C*
       a) hot dog   b) hamburger   c) toast
       d) apple pie   e) fries

11. **long jump**   **high jump**   hop   _a_
    a) skip   b) javelin   c) hammer throw
    d) sprint   e) freestyle

12. **up**   **down**   **beside**   _b_
    a) direct   b) around   c) instruction
    d) map   e) navigate

13. **dislike**   **disfavor**   **detract**   _c_
    a) endorse   b) like   c) discount
    d) approve   e) share

14. **river**   **stream**   **pond**   _e_
    a) lake   b) ocean   c) Earth
    d) mountain   e) rain

15. **ant**   **spider**   **beetle**   _d_
    a) wasp   d) fly   c) butterfly
    d) centipede   e) hornet

16. **brother**　　**father**　　**uncle**　　　_b_
    a) sister　　b) son　　c) grandmother
    d) mother　　e) daughter

17. **sponge**　　**crab**　　**jellyfish**　　_e_
    a) dog　　b) cat　　c) seagull
    d) snake　　e) seahorse

18. **bee**　　**wasp**　　**hornet**　　_a_
    a) locust　　b) grasshopper　　c) ant
    d) spider　　e) beetle

19. **English**　　**Spanish**　　**French**　　_c_
    a) South American　　b) Kansas　　c) German
    d) Iceland　　e) Native

20. **hamburger**　　**steak**　　**roast beef**　　_d_
    a) noodles　　b) fries　　c) ice cream
    d) hot dog　　e) rice

21. **Democracy**   **Fascism**   **Communism**   _a_
    a) Monarchy   b) Imperial   c) Empire
    d) Roman   e) Union

22. **liver**   **heart**   **lungs**   _d_
    a) skin   b) eyes   c) nose
    d) pancreas   e) toes

23. **Greece**   **Rome**   **Egypt**   _c_
    a) Viking   b) Assyrian   c) France
    d) Greenland   e) Japan

24. **worry**   **anger**   **fear**   _c_
    a) joy   b) ecstatic   c) sadness
    d) arrogant   e) alpha

25. **speak**   **sing**   **shout**   _d_
    a) shake   b) taxi   c) jog
    d) jam   e) coil

Verbal Classification: Answer Key

Question	Answer	Question	Answer
1	A	14	A
2	B	15	D
3	E	16	B
4	B	17	E
5	A	18	A
6	D	19	C
7	A	20	D
8	C	21	A
9	E	22	D
10	C	23	B
11	A	24	C
12	B	25	A
13	C		

There is no appendix for Verbal Classification explaining the correct answers. Review the answer sheet here and have a discussion on which questions were missed and what the correct answer is. **Some of these are intentionally hard**!

Language Skills: Verbal Analogies

This section has the familiar, "this word" is to "that word" as "other word" is to "[pick a word]". The only difference is the related words are separated by a |----------| instead of linking with the 'is to' 'as' words as you have probably seen before. So look at the first two words presented, figure out their relation, then look at the next word and pick a word from the answer set that has that same relation.

1.　　　　　　**day** |----------| **night**
　　　　　　　right |----------| _____

　　a) correct　　　　　　　b) happy　　　　　　　c) dark
　　d) sad　　　　　　　　　e) wrong

2.　　　　　　**camera** |----------| **eye**
　　　　　headphone |----------| _____

　　a) mouth　　　　　　　　b) nose　　　　　　　c) hand
　　d) eye　　　　　　　　　e) ear

3.　　　　　　**cloth** |----------| **thread**
　　　　　　　tank |----------| _____

　　a) fuel　　　　　　　　　b) tread　　　　　　　c) steel
　　d) engine　　　　　　　　e) gun

4.　　　　　　**wolf** |----------| **howl**
　　　　　children |----------| _____

　　a) play　　　　　　　　　b) scold　　　　　　　c) converse
　　d) dance　　　　　　　　e) sing

5.　　　　　　**car** |----------| **wheel**
　　　　　　camera |----------| _____

　　a) film　　　　　　　　　b) case　　　　　　　c) shutter
　　d) lenses　　　　　　　　e) strap

6.   fork |----------| food
            axe |----------| _____

a) wood   b) handle   c) stone
d) head   e) dirt

7.   couch |----------| pillow
          bed |----------| _____

a) rug   b) sheet   c) basket
d) canvas   e) curtain

8.   wood |----------| wood grain
    painting |----------| _____

a) paint   b) canvas   c) picture
d) color   e) brush stroke

9.   carpet |----------| shampoo
         car |----------| _____

a) wax   b) glass   c) paint
d) floor mat   e) gas

10.   paint |----------| canvas
     pencil |----------| _____

a) wall   b) lead   c) graphite
d) paper   e) poster

11.   soccer |----------| goal
      football |----------| _____
   a) basket   b) goal   c) score
   d) team   e) touchdown

12. **North America** |----------| **America**
      Europe |----------| _____
   a) South Africa   b) Germany   c) Morocco
   d) Berlin   e) London

13.   dog |----------| collar
      human |----------| _____
   a) hat   b) shirt   c) pants
   d) shoes   e) bowtie

14.   skull |----------| brain
      jar |----------| _____
   a) shelf   b) lid   c) glass
   d) pickles   e) clover

15.   fire pit |----------| smoke
      factory |----------| _____
   a) ash   b) cloud   c) coal
   d) smog   e) slag

16.   boxer |----------| **glove**
      woodsman |----------| _____
   a) log   b) truck   c) axe
   d) chain   e) hat

17.   music |----------| **song**
      philosophy |----------| _____
   a) class   b) Plato   c) socialism
   d) classification   e) argument

18.   herd |----------| **sheep**
      school |----------| _____
   a) fish   b) cattle   c) deer
   d) cats   e) wolves

19.   scissors |----------| **hair**
      telescope |----------| _____
   a) moon   b) laptop   c) smart phone
   d) mountain   e) camera

20.   washer |----------| **dryer**
      stove |----------| _____
   a) coffee maker   b) microwave   c) blender
   d) refrigerator   e) lawnmower

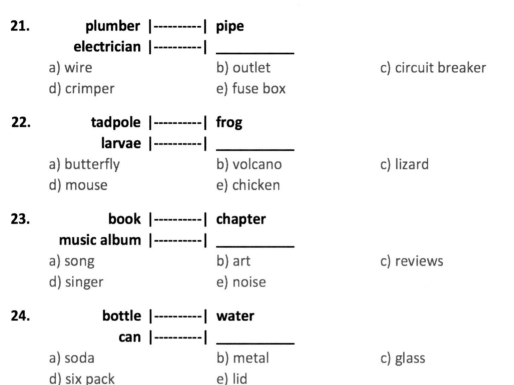

21.   plumber |----------| pipe
        electrician |----------| _____
    a) wire   b) outlet   c) circuit breaker
    d) crimper   e) fuse box

22.   tadpole |----------| frog
        larvae |----------| _____
    a) butterfly   b) volcano   c) lizard
    d) mouse   e) chicken

23.   book |----------| chapter
        music album |----------| _____
    a) song   b) art   c) reviews
    d) singer   e) noise

24.   bottle |----------| water
        can |----------| _____
    a) soda   b) metal   c) glass
    d) six pack   e) lid

End Of Section!
Keep Up The Good Work!

Verbal Analogies: Answer Key

Question	Answer	Question	Answer
1	E	13	E
2	E	14	D
3	C	15	D
4	E	16	C
5	A	17	E
6	A	18	A
7	B	19	A
8	E	20	B
9	A	21	A
10	D	22	A
11	E	23	A
12	B	24	A

There is no appendix for Verbal Analogies explaining the correct answers. Review the answer sheet here and have a discussion on which questions were missed and what the correct answer is.

Tips for the test:
- The first word pairs are RELATED in different ways
  - Word A is similar to Word B (such as miniscule |-| small)
  - Word A is opposite to Word B (such as Make |-| Destroy)
  - Word A is a part of Word B (such as key |-| piano)

First find the RELATION then use elimination method to find that same RELATION.

Appendix A: Figure Pattern Answer Guide

Here we explain each question and answer found in the Figure Pattern quiz. The answer is found in the text under the question.

Figure Pattern: Question 1

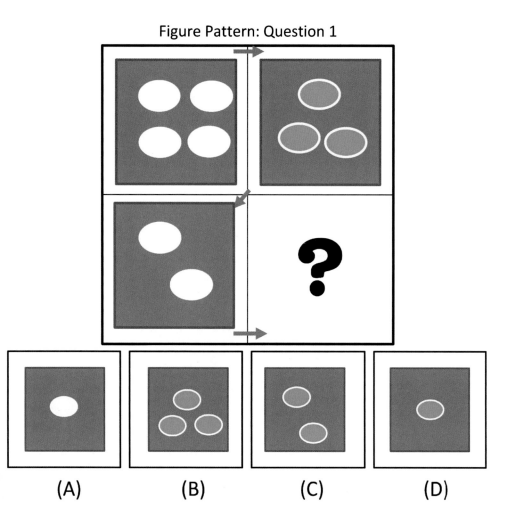

(A)   (B)   (C)   (D)

We can see that each picture has one less circle, and that we have 2 white circle squares and one with green circles. It appears that even numbers of circles are white and odd numbers are green. D is the best answer because it has 1 circle and it is green.

Figure Pattern: Question 2

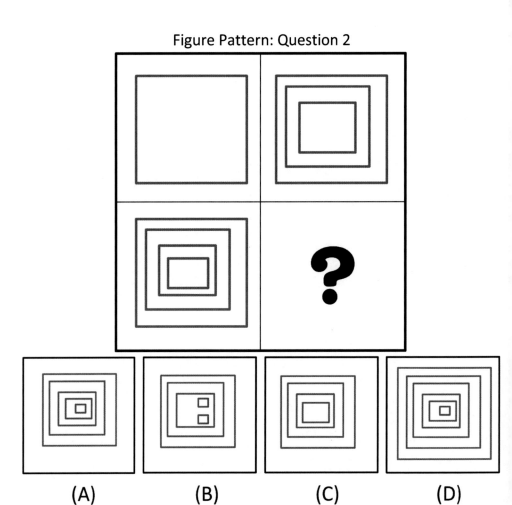

(A)   (B)   (C)   (D)

This pattern moves from left to right in the example pictures. The square on the top left gets two more squares added inside of it. Take the bottom left square and add two more squares inside of it. The answer is D. You can also do this by counting the total number of squares and adding two to it. The bottom left picture has 4 squares. Answer D has 6 squares. Answer A & B have 5 squares. Answer C has 4 squares.

Figure Pattern: Question 3

(A)   (B)   (C)   (D)

The shapes in this question don't matter. Watch the change in color and the
dotted lines from left to right. The top left has 1 line and is blue. Then there are 2
more lines and the shape is red. The bottom left has 4 lines and is blue. If we add
two lines and change the color we are looking for a red shape with six lines.
Answer C is the only answer that fits this.

Figure Pattern: Question 4

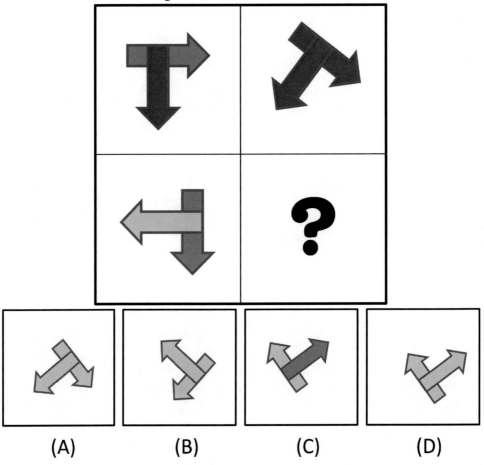

(A)   (B)   (C)   (D)

This pattern makes you pay attention to the rotation and color change of the shape. In the top left red arrow on top of blue arrow turns into two red arrows that rotate to the right slightly. Bottom left we have green arrow on blue arrow that will rotate right slightly and become two green arrows. Answer B does this. Answer C is not all green and answers A and D are rotated in the wrong direction or rotated too much.

Figure Pattern: Question 5

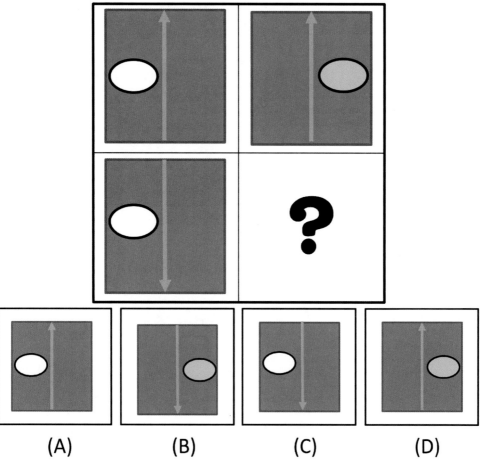

(A) (B) (C) (D)

In the top pictures we see an arrow pointing up with a white circle on the left and then a green circle on the right. On the bottom, we see the same picture as the top except the arrow is going down. The best answer is B, because it reverses the arrow from the top picture with a green circle.

Figure Pattern: Question 6

(A)   (B)   (C)   (D)

For this question we see that the top and bottom left squares are exactly the same. When we look at our answers, B and D look like they might fit. D has the colors reversed, and B is the same. Judging from the left side pictures, B is the best answer because it is the same as the one above it.

Figure Pattern: Question 7

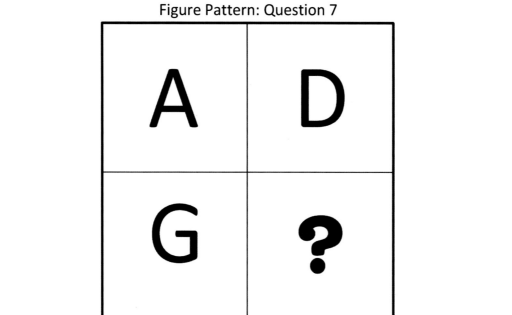

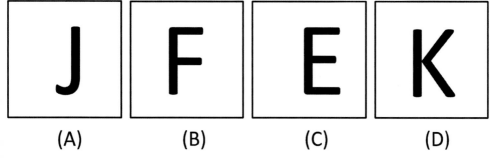

(A)   (B)   (C)   (D)

How can we pick between these letters? If we read the squares from left to right, and we count the letters between A and D we get 2 skipped letters. If we skip 2 letters after G we end up on J. A is the correct answer.

Figure Pattern: Question 8

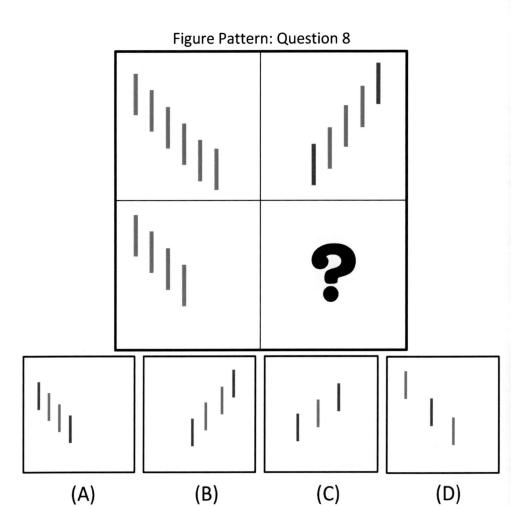

(A)   (B)   (C)   (D)

Let's read the squares from left to right again. On the top, we have 6 blue lines and in the next picture there are 5 lines (1 less) climbing up rather than down with a red line at the beginning and end. Now let's do this same process on the bottom: make the lines climb up instead of down, subtract one line, and turn the first and last one red. This perfectly matches C, and it is the correct answer.

Figure Pattern: Question 9

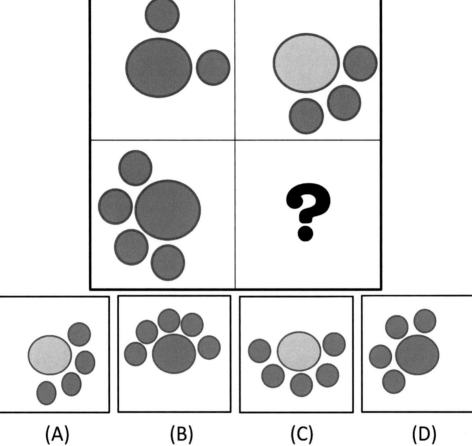

(A) (B) (C) (D)

In each square we are adding 1 circle and alternating yellow to blue for the big circle. B and C both have the correct number of small circles, but B has another blue large circle. C is the better answer because it has 5 small circles and a big yellow circle.

Figure Pattern: Question 10

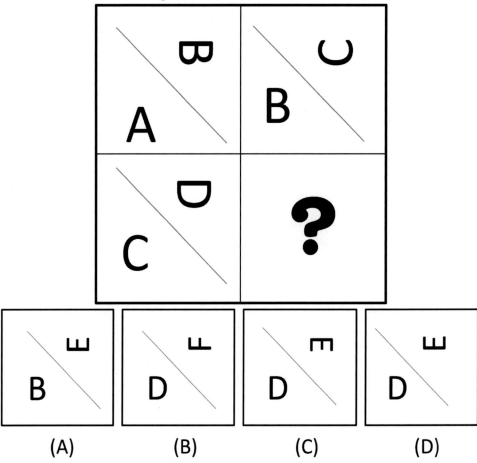

(A)   (B)   (C)   (D)

Look at the top 2 squares. What is happening is the letter on the top right corner is moving to the bottom left corner, and then the top right corner is being replaced by the next letter in the alphabet. Or you can just think about both letters going to the next letter in the alphabet, and then the top right letter changes positions to be facing "up". So C turns into D, and D turns into E. Is the answer C or D? The answer is D because the E is facing "up".

Figure Pattern: Question 11

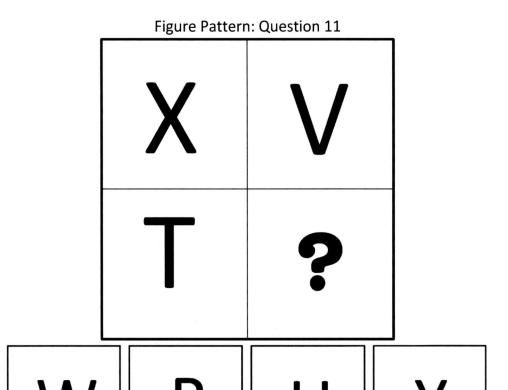

X	V
T	?

(A)	(B)	(C)	(D)
W	R	U	Y

Look at the top row. If you sing the alphabet song in your head, you will realize that if we go backwards 2 letters from X, we get V. What letter is 2 letters backwards from T? R. The correct answer is B.

Figure Pattern: Question 12

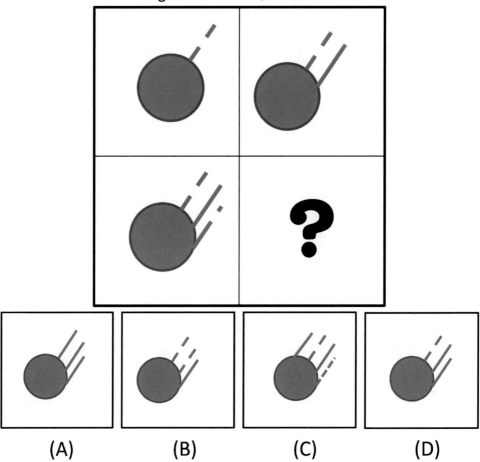

(A)   (B)   (C)   (D)

At first glance it looks like the type of line coming out of the circle will be important. In reality though, the only thing that is important is the number of lines. Each square has one additional line coming out of the circle, which means we should be looking for 4 lines. The answer is C.

Figure Pattern: Question 13

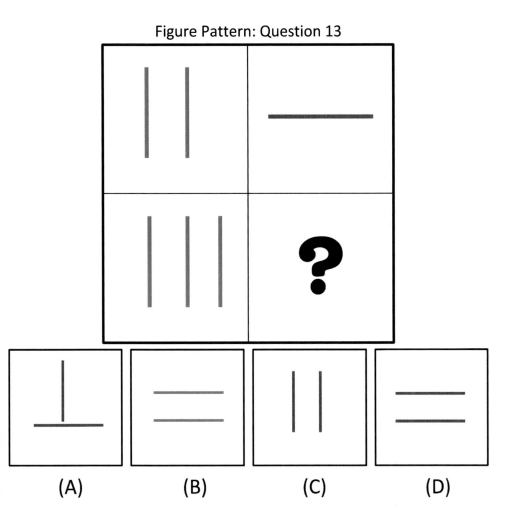

(A)   (B)   (C)   (D)

In the top row, we subtract one line, turn it red, and turn it sideways. If we try this on the bottom row, we should expect 2 red lines going horizontally. D is the correct answer.

Figure Pattern: Question 14

On the top we see that the line goes to the bottom and the circle changes colors. On the bottom, the line starts on the left side instead of the right, so we can guess that the line probably shouldn't move to the bottom like it did before. Looking at our answers, that eliminates C, which is the same answer. B must be the correct answer because it is the only one left that has the correct color.

Figure Pattern: Question 15

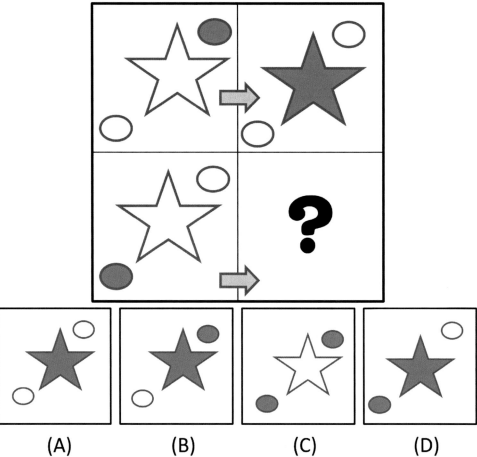

(A)   (B)   (C)   (D)

In the top row, the star turns blue and the blue circle turns white. What should happen on the bottom? The star should definitely turn blue, so that eliminates answer C. On the top the circle turned white not blue, so we should expect 2 white circles. We end up with the same thing as the top, which is A.

Figure Pattern: Question 16

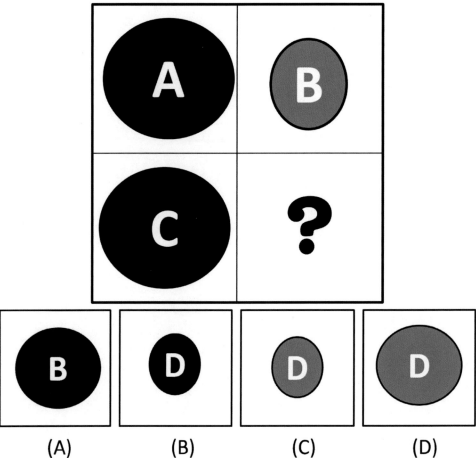

(A)   (B)   (C)   (D)

When you see A, B, C you probably immediately thought D was next. Three of your answers have a D in them, but which one is correct? On the top a large black circle turns into a smaller blue circle, so on the bottom we should expect the same thing. We are looking for a smaller blue circle with a D in it. C is the correct answer.

Figure Pattern: Question 17

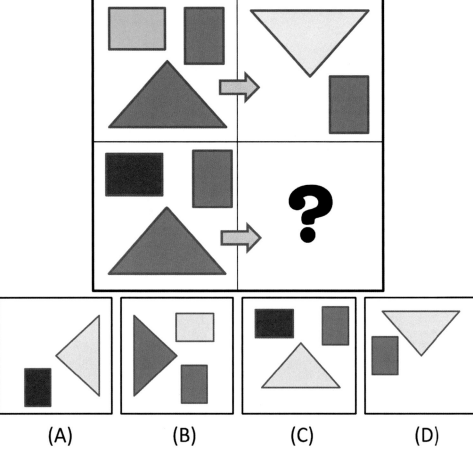

(A)　　　　　(B)　　　　　(C)　　　　　(D)

In the top row we delete the non-blue rectangle, flip the triangle upside down, and turn it yellow. If we try the on the bottom, we would expect the same answer as the top. None of our answers match the top though, so we need to look for the best one. A and B have the triangle pointing different directions, and C has too many colors and rectangles. D looks like the best answer.

Figure Pattern: Question 18

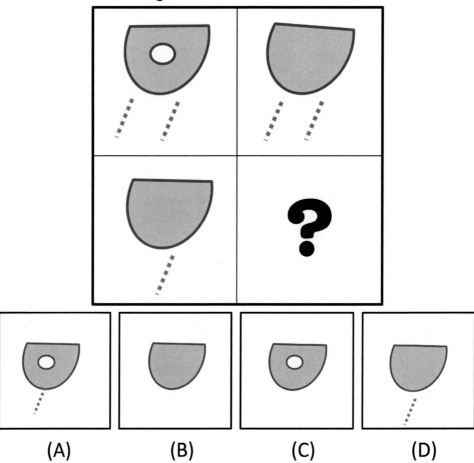

(A)   (B)   (C)   (D)

This pattern goes from left to right and from top right to bottom left in a series of 3 pictures. After each change of picture one thing is removed from the picture. From top left to top right the circle is removed. From top right to bottom left one of the dotted lines is removed. In the next picture we should see another piece removed. Answer B is a picture with the last dotted line removed.

Figure Pattern: Question 19

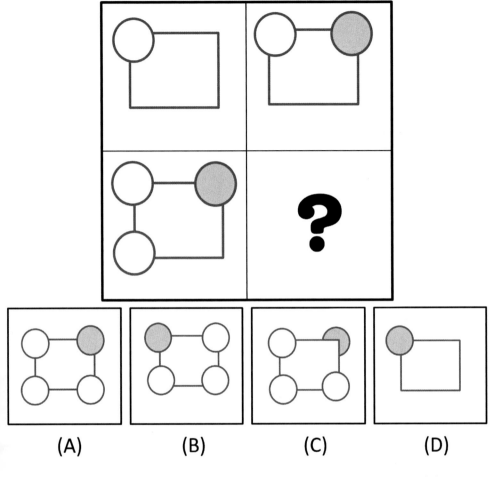

(A)   (B)   (C)   (D)

In each one of these squares we are adding an additional circle to a corner of the rectangle, so in our answer we should look for a rectangle with a circle on each corner. That eliminates answers C and D. Between A and B, A is the easy choice because none of our example squares have the yellow circle on the left side. A is the best answer.

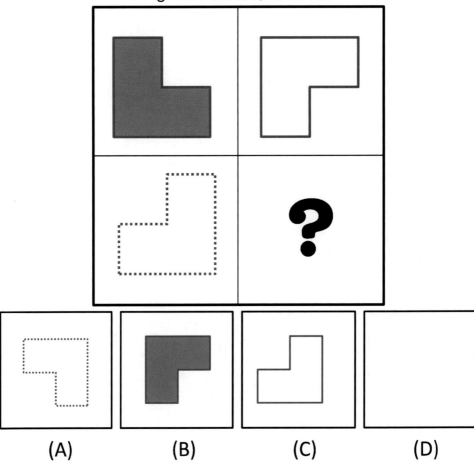

(A)   (B)   (C)   (D)

This question works from top left to top right and then from top right to bottom left. Like in Question 18 each time the picture changes something is taken away. We go from a full blue to just a line in the top two pictures. In the bottom picture we go from dotted line to nothing. Answer D wins. This picture is deliberately confusing to push the boundary of what you think an acceptable answer may be.

Figure Pattern: Question 21

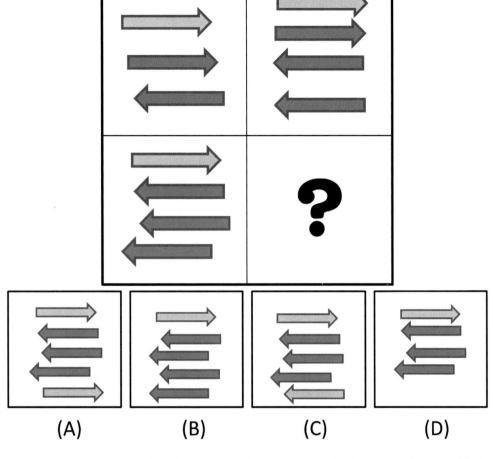

(A)   (B)   (C)   (D)

In the top row, it looks like a blue arrow that points to the left is just being added to the bottom. If we try this on the bottom, we should get a yellow arrow pointing to the right followed by 4 blue arrows leading to the left. B is the correct answer.

Figure Pattern: Question 22

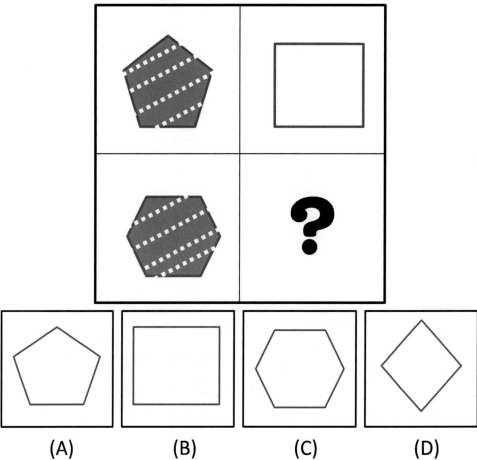

(A)   (B)   (C)   (D)

In the top row, we change from a five sided to a 4-sided shape, remove the dotted lines, and remove the blue color. If we do the same thing on the bottom, we should go from a 6 sided to a 5-sided shape that is empty on the inside. A is the correct answer.

Figure Pattern: Question 23

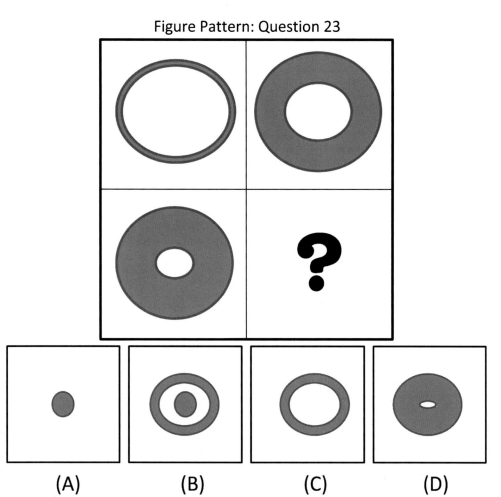

(A)   (B)   (C)   (D)

In the top row, the only thing that happens is the big white circle shrinks to a smaller circle. If we shrink the white circle even more it will be very small. D is the best answer.

Figure Pattern: Question 24

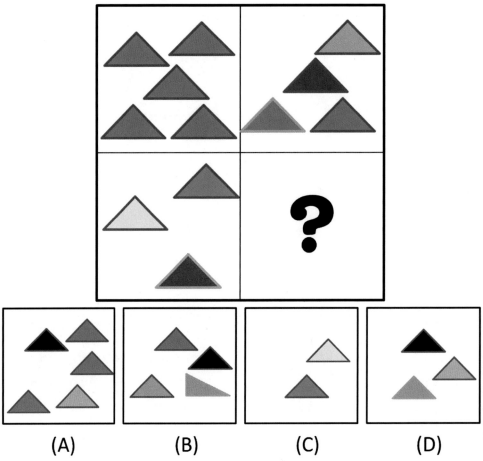

(A) (B) (C) (D)

Don't be distracted on this one by the colors; we can solve it just by counting triangles. In each square we have one less triangle. C is the best answer because it has 2 triangles.

Figure Pattern: Question 25

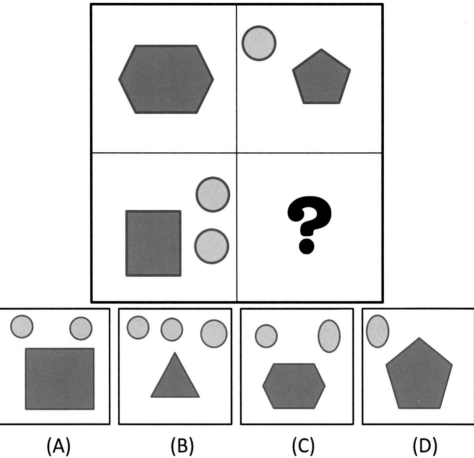

(A)   (B)   (C)   (D)

Compare the squares on top. We lose one side from our shape (6 sides to 5 sides) and we add a circle. On the bottom then, we should end up with a triangle and 3 circles. B is the correct answer.

Appendix B: Figure Matrices Answer Guide
Figure Matrices: Question 1

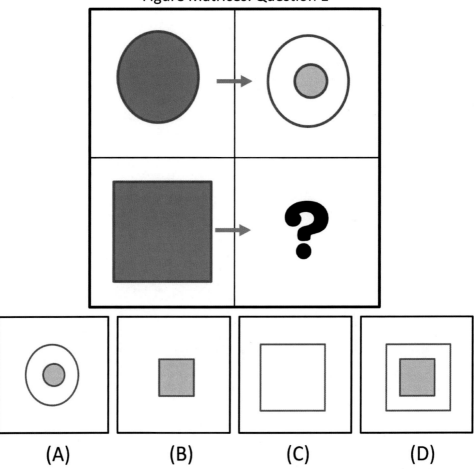

(A) (B) (C) (D)

The circle turns white, and an additional yellow circle is added to the middle. On the bottom, we should expect the square to turn white and an additional yellow square to be added to the middle. D is the correct answer.

Figure Matrices: Question 2

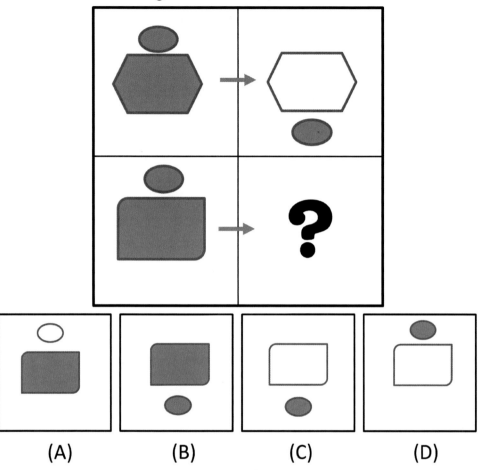

(A)   (B)   (C)   (D)

The blue circle moves from the top to the bottom, and the solid blue shape turns white. C is the correct answer.

Figure Matrices: Question 3

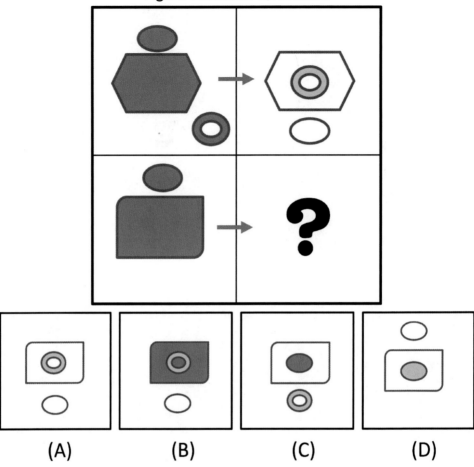

(A)   (B)   (C)   (D)

This one is a little trickier because we just have to find the best answer. We can tell that the blue circle should move to the bottom, and that the big shape should turn white. B and D are eliminated because the big shape doesn't change color in B, and in D the circle doesn't move to the bottom. The bottom picture doesn't have a blue circle in the bottom right like the top one does, but when we look at A and C we have to eliminate C because it puts a green circle on the bottom where we expect the blue circle to be. That leaves A as the best answer.

Figure Matrices: Question 4

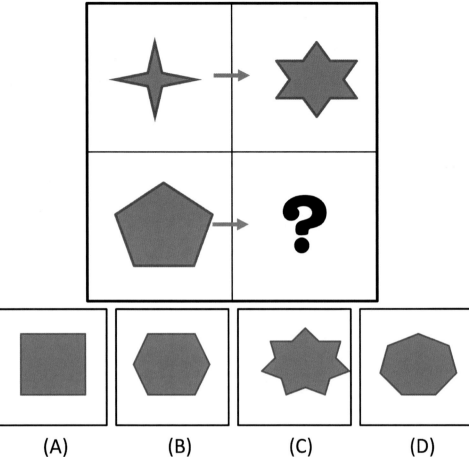

(A)   (B)   (C)   (D)

In this question a star with 4 points turns into a star with 6 points. It looks like we can just add 2 points. On the bottom we have a 5-sided shape. If we add 2 we should expect a 7-sided shape. C has 7 points and D has 7 sides. D is the best answer because although C has 7 points, it doesn't have 7 sides.

Figure Matrices: Question 5

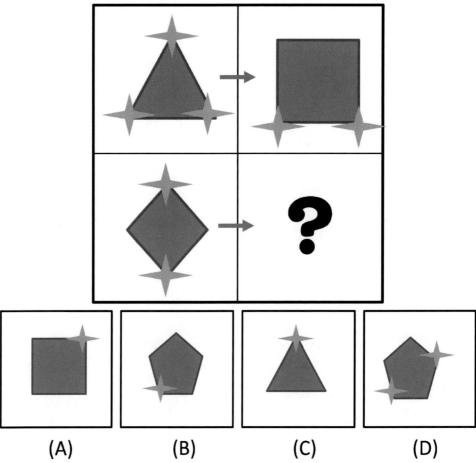

(A) (B) (C) (D)

In the top row the top star is removed and the shape adds a side going from a triangle to a square. If we add a side to the bottom, we get a 5-sided shape. That narrows us down to B or D. We also need to remove the star from the top, so that means the best answer is B.

Figure Matrices: Question 6

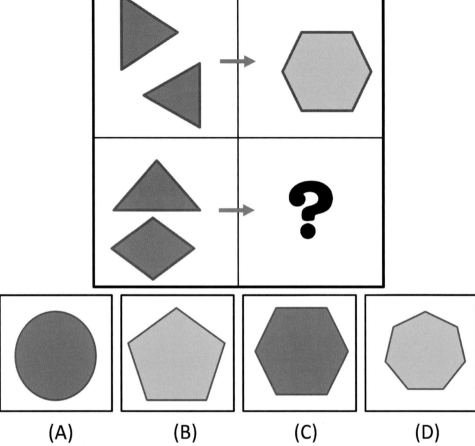

(A)　　　　　(B)　　　　　(C)　　　　　(D)

It is easy to see that our answer should be green, but which shape do we pick? In the top row we have 2 objects with 3 sides that combine into an object with 6 sides. On the bottom we have an object with 3 sides and an object with 4 sides, so we should expect an answer with 7 sides. D is the correct answer.

Figure Matrices: Question 7

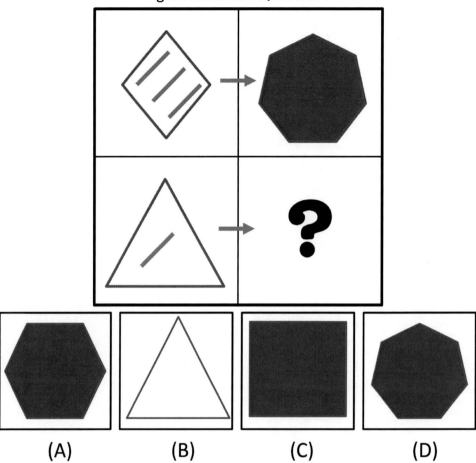

(A)   (B)   (C)   (D)

In this one we know we need a red shape for our answer, but that only eliminates B as a correct answer. What is happening here is the lines on the inside of the shape are being added as sides to the object. So on the top we have a diamond with 3 lines, which means we are looking for 4 + 3 = 7 sides in the answer. On the bottom we have a triangle (3 sides) with 1 line, so 3 + 1 = 4 sides for the answer. C is the correct answer because it has 4 sides.

Figure Matrices: Question 8

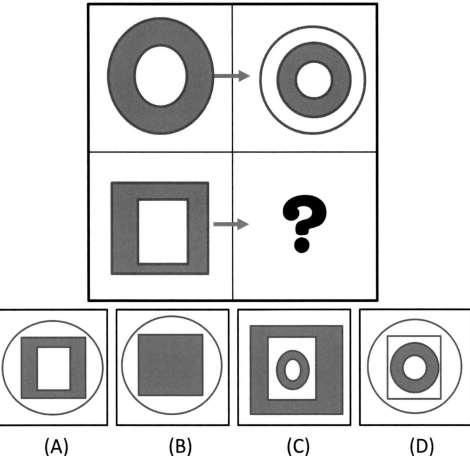

(A)   (B)   (C)   (D)

In the top row it looks like we are just adding another shape around the existing shapes. In the bottom row we should look for the same shape with a big square around it. That's not one of our answers though, which means that in the top row we weren't adding another of the same shape, we were just adding a big circle. If we add a big circle to the bottom square, we get that A is the correct answer.

Figure Matrices: Question 9

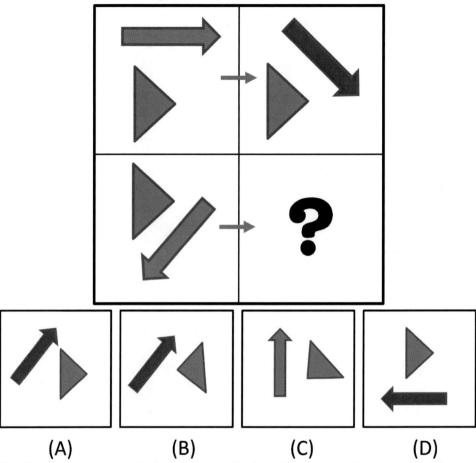

(A)   (B)   (C)   (D)

The first thing to notice is that the triangle doesn't move or change at all. That means we can eliminate B and C as possible answers. Between A and D, D is the better answer because the arrow only moves a little way around the square. Answer A has the arrow moving to the opposite side, which isn't what happens in the top row. D is the correct answer.

Figure Matrices: Question 10

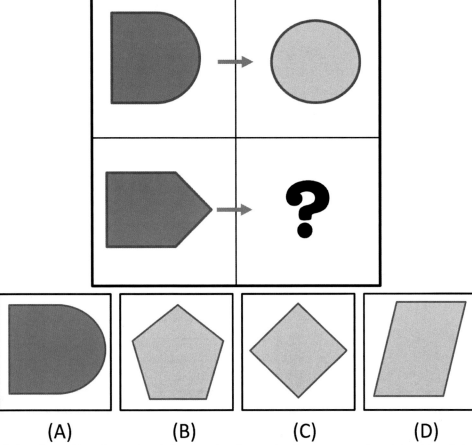

(A)   (B)   (C)   (D)

It's hard to tell at first what is happening here. In the top row the right side of the object stays the same. So, if we chop off the left side of the object on the bottom row and put what is on the right side of the object on the left, we end up with a diamond. C is the correct answer.

Figure Matrices: Question 11

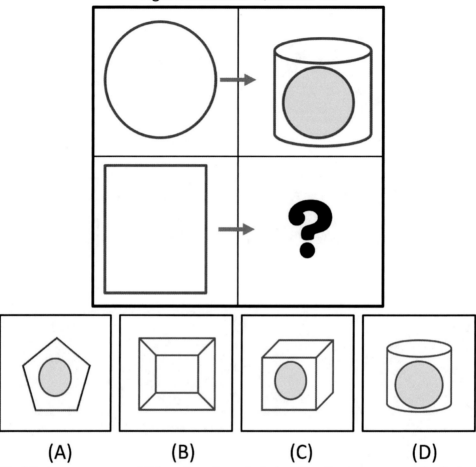

(A) (B) (C) (D)

All of the answers except B have a yellow circle just like the top row, so the first thing we can do is eliminate B as an answer. D is the same as the answer on the top so we can safely eliminate it as well. C is the best remaining answer. What is happening here is the shape on the left is turning into a 3D shape on the right. The circle is turning into a cylinder with a yellow circle in it, and on the bottom the square is turning into a cube with a yellow circle in it. C is the correct answer.

Figure Matrices: Question 12

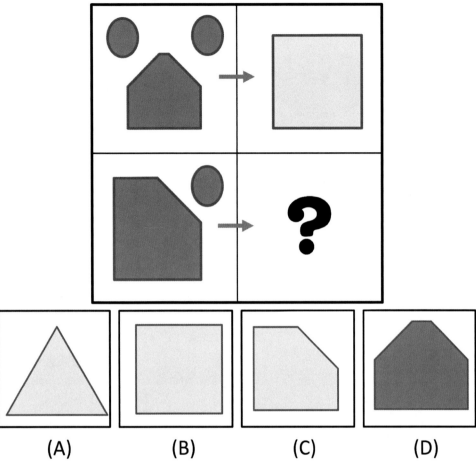

(A) (B) (C) (D)

In this question the 2 blue circles are being "added" to the shape to fill in the corners. On the bottom, if we add in the single circle we should get a square. On the top the object turns yellow, so we also should turn it yellow on the bottom. B is the correct answer.

Figure Matrices: Question 13

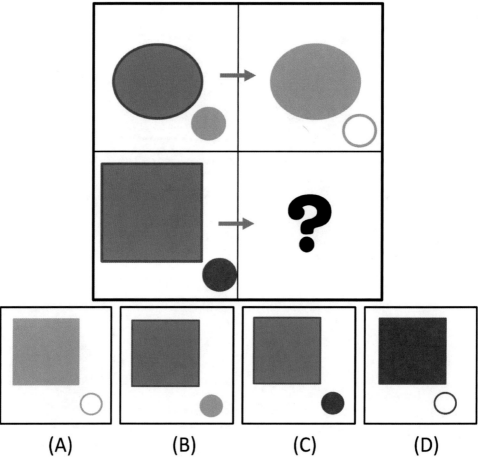

(A) (B) (C) (D)

In this question, the color of the small circle is filling the larger circle, leaving it empty. In the bottom row, we should "fill" the square with the red color. This will leave an empty red circle on the bottom right. D is the correct answer.

Figure Matrices: Question 14

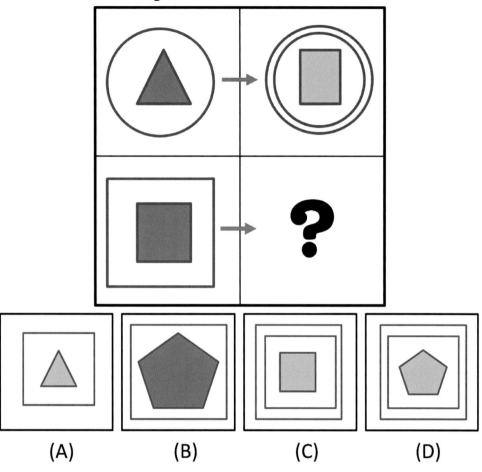

(A)   (B)   (C)   (D)

In this question several things are being modified. The object is being changed to a green color, an additional shape is being drawn around the outside (1 circle to 2 circles in the top row), and an additional side is being added to the object (triangle to square). If we make all of these modifications on the bottom, we get a green shape, an additional square on the outside, and our square with 4 sides into a shape with 5 sides. D is the correct answer.

Figure Matrices: Question 15

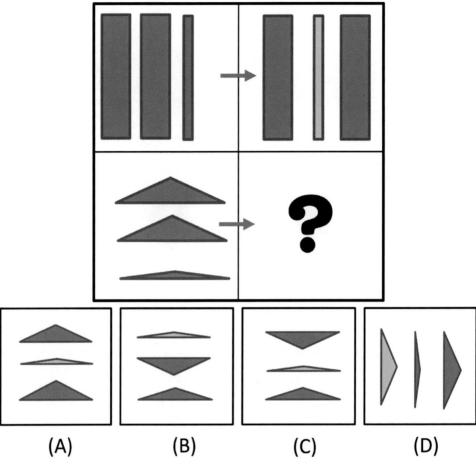

(A)   (B)   (C)   (D)

In the top row the skinniest shape is being moved to the middle and turned green. If we move the skinniest shape to the middle and turn it green in the bottom square, we narrow down our possible answers to A or C. A is correct it maintains the original directions that the triangles are pointing in.

Figure Matrices: Question 16

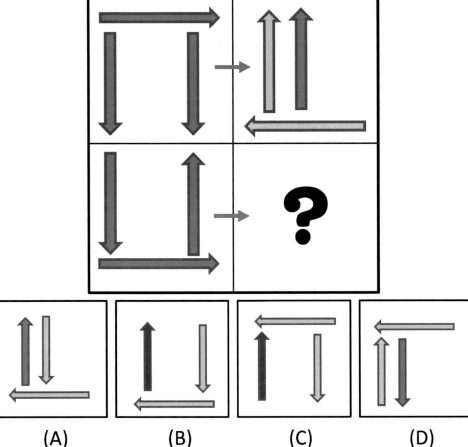

(A) (B) (C) (D)

Let's use the process of elimination on this one. The first thing we see that happens is the horizontal arrow on the top moves to the bottom. On the bottom square then, we need to move the arrow on the bottom to the top. That narrows down our answer to C or D. You can see that in the top row the original blue color is maintained for one of the other 2 arrows. Also, the arrows arranged vertically start out on the left and right sides, but then are moved and squished together on the left side. D is the best answer.

Figure Matrices: Question 17

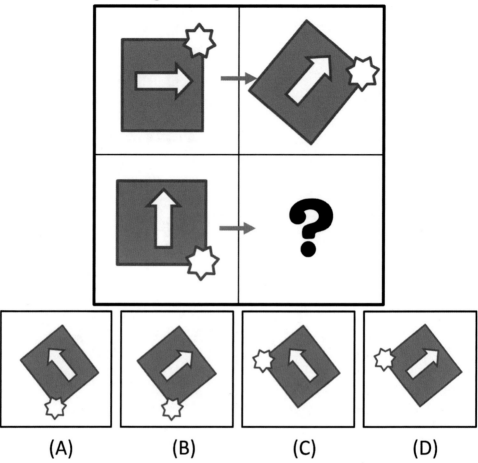

In the top row the arrow rotates counter clockwise. If we rotate the arrow on the bottom counter clockwise it will be in the position of answers A and C. Now look at the star shape. It seems to rotate a little bit in the opposite direction. A is the best answer because the star in C moves to far to the other side.

Figure Matrices: Question 18

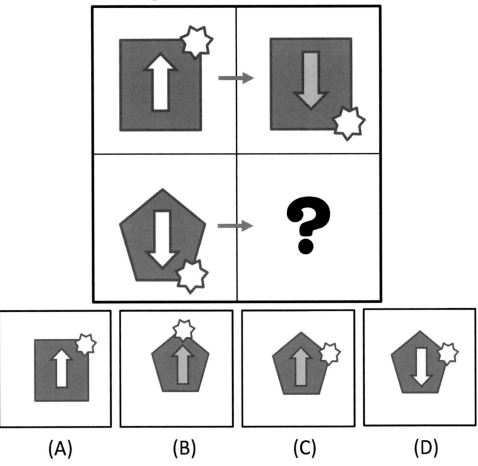

(A)   (B)   (C)   (D)

In the top row the arrow turns upside down and changes to a yellow color. That narrows down the answer to either B or C. In answer B, the star goes to the very top, and in answer C the star stays on one side of the pentagon but goes to the top. C is the best answer, because in the top row the star doesn't go to the center, it goes to the center right.

Figure Matrices: Question 19

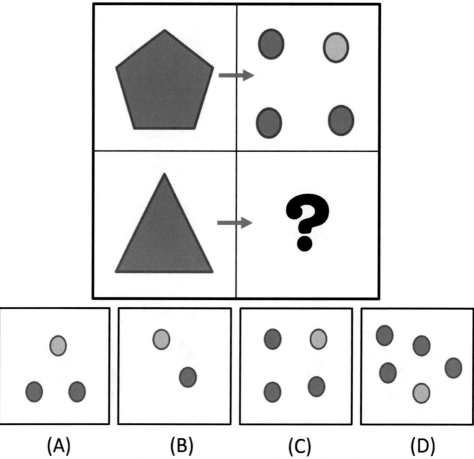

(A)   (B)   (C)   (D)

This is another question based on how many sides the object has. On the top, an object with 5 sides turns into 4 circles. That means that on the bottom, the shape with 3 sides should turn into 2 circles. B is the best answer.

Figure Matrices: Question 20

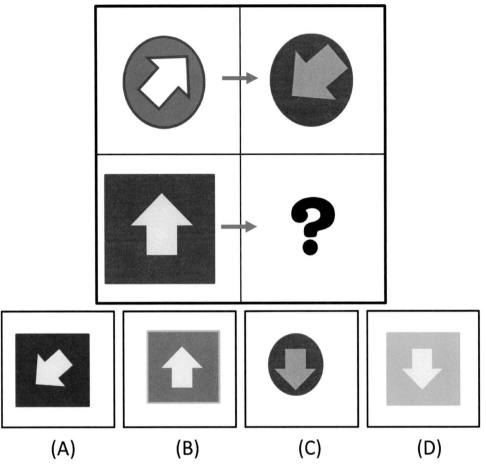

(A)   (B)   (C)   (D)

In the top row, the arrow goes the opposite direction and both the circle and the arrow change colors. Only C and D are pointing the opposite way, and C can be eliminated because the red color didn't change. D must be the correct answer.

Figure Matrices: Question 21

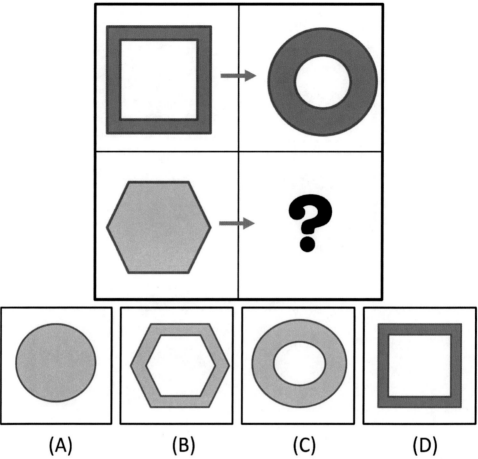

(A)   (B)   (C)   (D)

What is happening in the top row? The only thing that is changing is that the shapes are turning into circles. There is only one shape in the bottom row, and if we turn it into a circle A is the correct answer.

Figure Matrices: Question 22

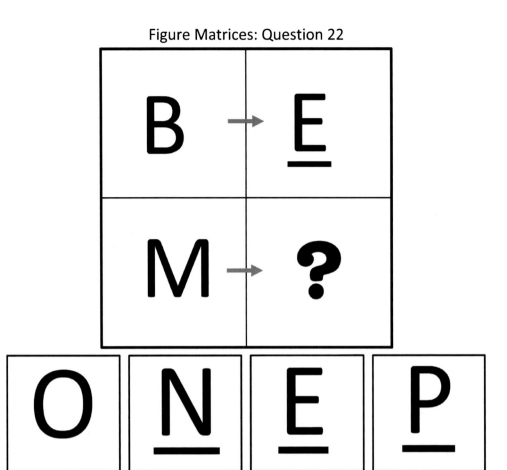

(A)   (B)   (C)   (D)

In this question the letter is just advancing 3 more letters through the alphabet and then it is underlined. 3 Letters past M is P, so D is the correct answer.

Figure Matrices: Question 23

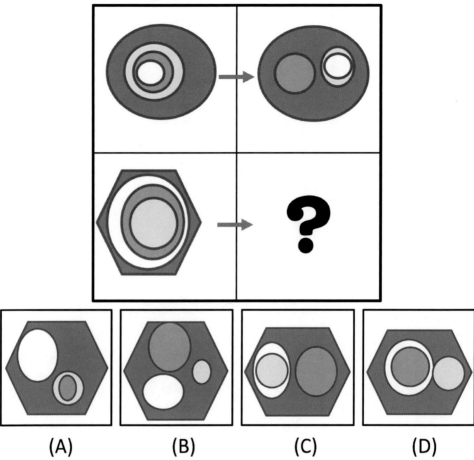

(A)   (B)   (C)   (D)

The blue shape is staying the same in this question. Then the smallest circle is separated out into the biggest circle. If we follow this logic, we should see the biggest circle (white) with the smallest circle (yellow) in it. Then the peach colored circle is left the same. Only C has a yellow circle in a white circle, which means that it is the correct answer.

Figure Matrices: Question 24

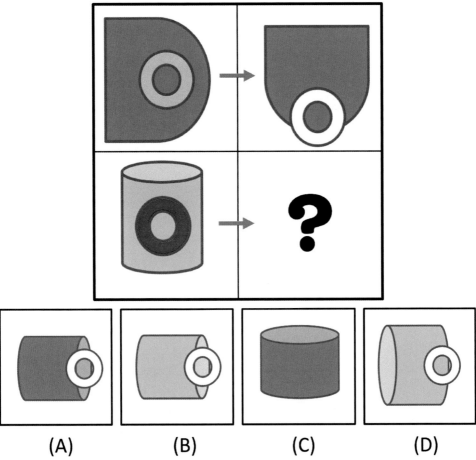

(A)   (B)   (C)   (D)

In the top row, the big shape is rotated and the smaller shape is turned white and pushed to the edge of the big shape. B is the correct answer because answer D has the white circle on the wrong side and the other answers are the wrong color.

Figure Matrices: Question 25

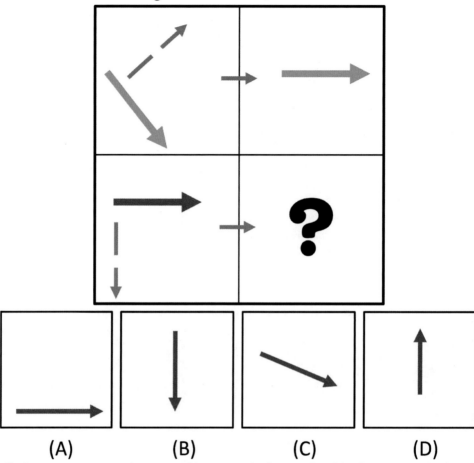

(A)   (B)   (C)   (D)

All of our answers just have a red line, so which way should it be pointing? This question asks you to think about the effect one shape has on another. In the top left picture, the green arrow is pointing diagonally downward. The blue line is pointing upwards. Then we see the green arrow pointing to the right. It is as if the blue line 'pulled' the green line in a different direction. In the bottom left we see the red line and the blue line 'pulling' it down. How far down? Well in the top example the blue line was able to 'pull' it about 45 degrees. So Answer C shows the red line 'pulled' about 45 degrees downward.

Appendix C: Paper Folding Answer Guide
Paper Folding: Question 1

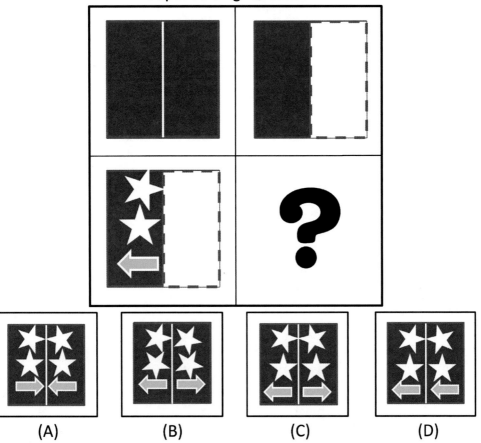

(A)   (B)   (C)   (D)

When you fold a horizontal arrow it will be pointing the opposite direction, so the answer must be B or C. B can be eliminated because the star in the middle is tilted on both sides of the paper when it should be straight. C is the correct answer.

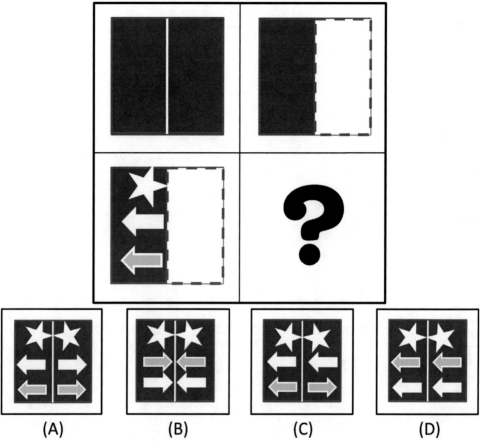

(A)   (B)   (C)   (D)

All of the arrows will be pointing the opposite direction when unfolded. That means that A must be the correct answer, because all of the other answers have arrows going the wrong direction.

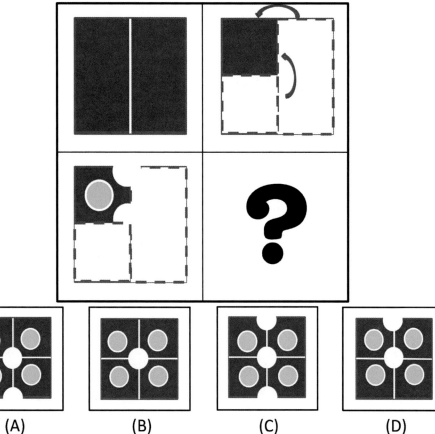

(A)   (B)   (C)   (D)

All of the answers correctly have a green circle in the middle of each square, and a circle right in the middle. We also need to look for a half circle at the top and bottom of the paper, which means that C is the correct answer.

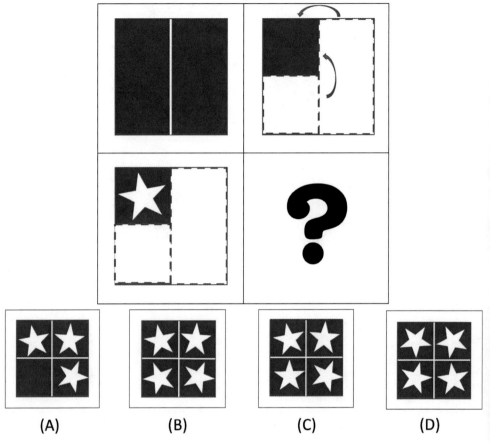

(A)   (B)   (C)   (D)

In this question, look at how the star is pointing towards the center of the page. When you unfold the paper you should see four stars pointing towards the center of the page. Answer B is the best representation of this.

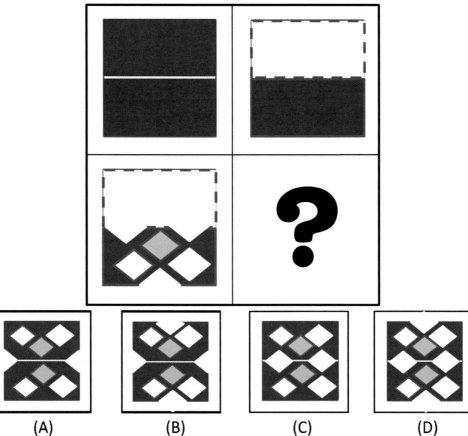

The half diamonds in the center of the paper will become full diamonds when unfolded, and that narrows down our answer to C or D. C can be eliminated because it is missing the half diamond at the bottom and top. D is the correct answer.

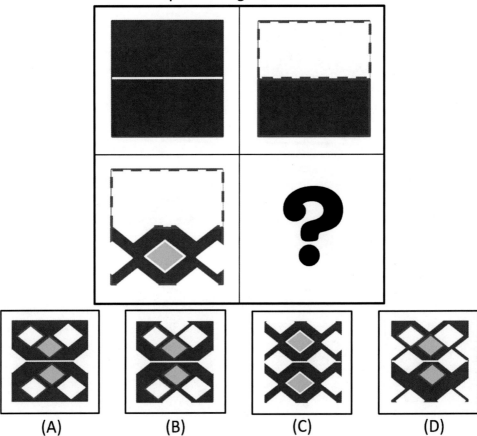

(A)   (B)   (C)   (D)

This is an easy question if you look at the green diamond – note that it has a white outline. Only C has that white outline, so it must be correct.

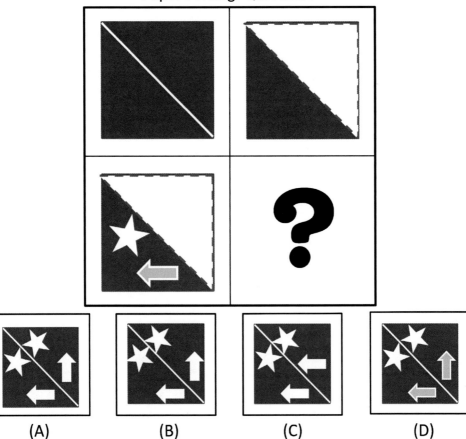

(A)   (B)   (C)   (D)

When we unfold a paper diagonally that has an arrow, the arrow will change direction. That means that C cannot be correct. If you look at the colors, however, you can immediately tell that D must be correct, because the other options have no color.

Paper Folding: Question 8

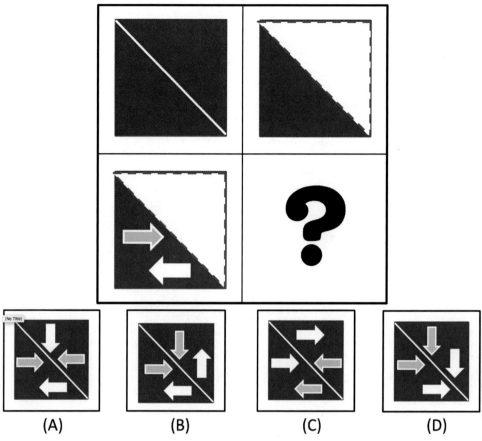

When this is unfolded diagonally, the green arrow will end up pointing down, and the white arrow will be pointing up. B is the correct answer.

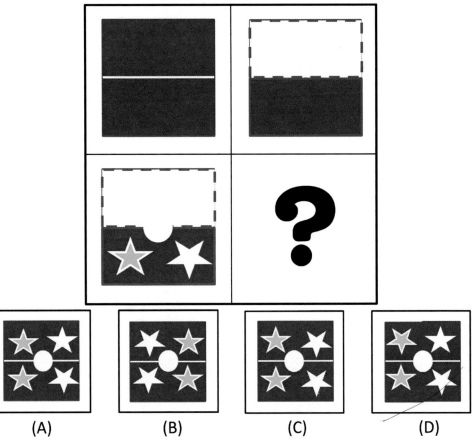

Look at the green arrow first. It is not tilted, so we should expect it to be perfectly upside down when the paper is unfolded. When folded, the green arrow points straight up, so it should end up pointing straight down. D must be the correct answer.

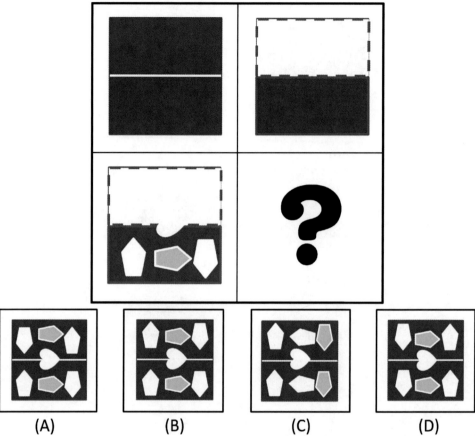

(A)   (B)   (C)   (D)

The arrow shapes pointing up and down will reverse directions when the paper is unfolded. So on top we should see an arrow pointing down, a green arrow pointed right, and then an arrow pointing up. That narrows it down to A or D. D is wrong because the initial positioning of the shapes on the bottom is wrong. A is the correct answer.

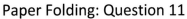

Paper Folding: Question 11

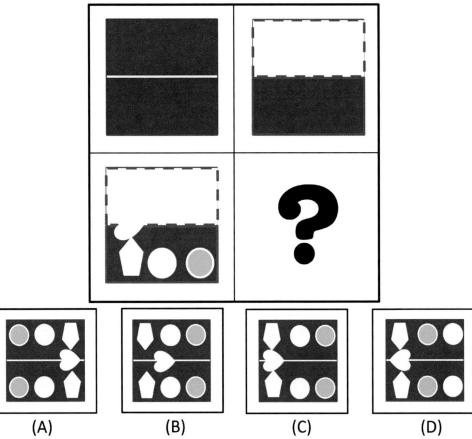

(A)   (B)   (C)   (D)

When the paper is unfolded the circles won't change. The arrow will be upside down, and the half heart will turn into a full heart. A, B, and D all have the heart in the wrong place or facing the wrong way, so C must be correct.

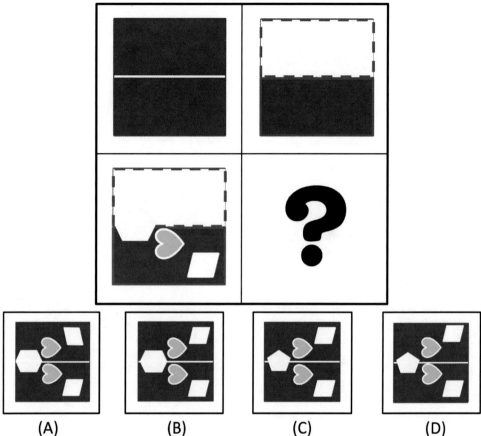

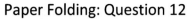

(A)   (B)   (C)   (D)

The object we want to pay the closest attention to is the 4-sided shape that is slanted. When it is flipped upside down, it will not be leaning the same direction. B, C, and D all have that shape leaning the same way, so A must be correct.

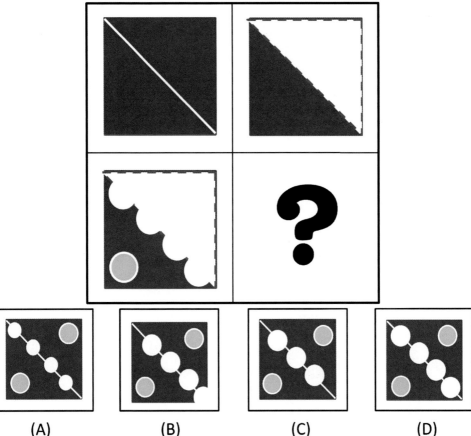

(A)	(B)	(C)	(D)

The 4 half circles will all turn into full circles, and we should expect a green circle in the opposite corner. C can be eliminated because it doesn't have enough circles, and B can be eliminated because the circle on the furthest right is pushed too far down. Between A and D, the circles in A are too skinny, which means D must be the correct answer.

Paper Folding: Question 14

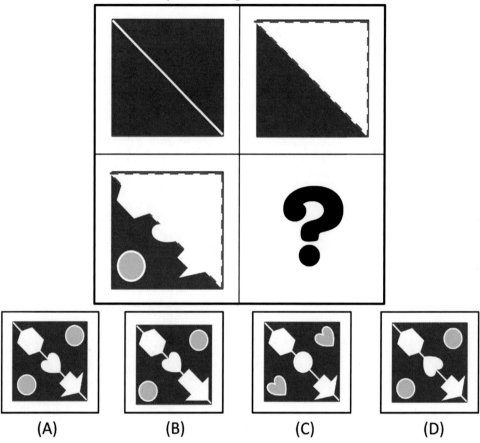

(A)   (B)   (C)   (D)

Let's use the process of elimination again. C is wrong because it has hearts instead of circles. B is wrong because the arrow is too fat. D is wrong because the heart is pointing the wrong way. That leaves only A, which is the correct answer.

Paper Folding: Question 15

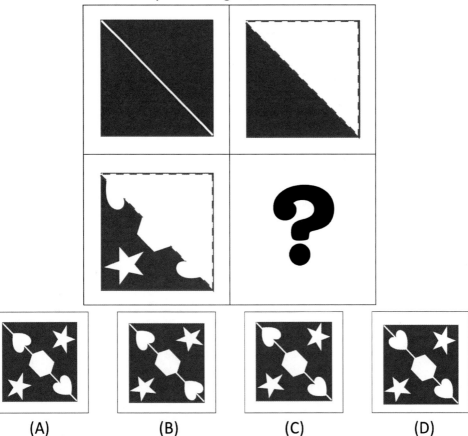

(A) (B) (C) (D)

Once again we can use the process of elimination. The hearts in B and D are going the wrong way. The bottom left star in A is pointing the wrong starting direction, which means that C must be the correct answer.

Paper Folding: Question 16

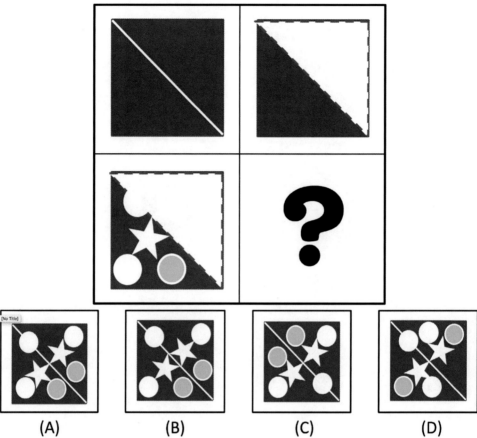

(A)   (B)   (C)   (D)

We can immediately eliminate C and D because the green circles are in the wrong place. If you look at the star, you can see that the top of the star has 2 points almost touching the folding line. The star in A is rotated somewhat and has only 1 point touching the line. That means that B must be the correct answer.

Appendix D: Number Series Tips

A number series is a sequence of numbers that have a logical pattern. In this section we will train you up on some tips on how to recognize the pattern and find the best answer.

Let's start easy, can you identify the next number?

$$1 \quad 2 \quad 3 \quad 4 \quad \underline{\hspace{2em}}$$

The next number is of course 5. Why do you know that it is 5 though? You know it is 5 because you can tell that you are counting by 1, or always doing + 1.

When you do harder patterns, you can sometimes still ask yourself, "What number am I adding each time?" Try this one:

$$1 \quad 3 \quad 5 \quad 7 \quad \underline{\hspace{2em}}$$

The next number is 9. This time you were just thinking "+2" after each number.

Now try this:

$$1 \quad 1 \quad 2 \quad 3 \quad 5 \quad 8 \quad \underline{\hspace{2em}}$$

If you said the next number is 11 then you would be wrong. The correct answer is 13. In this example, we aren't adding the same number each time, so you have to remind yourself to always check the whole pattern. We are actually always adding the previous 2 numbers together to get the next number. This is a common pattern you need to recognize in math. So the pattern goes 1 + nothing is still 1, giving you your first 2 numbers 1 1. Then 1 + 1 = 2, so now your pattern is 1 1 2. Then 1 + 2 = 3 so now are pattern is 1 1 2 3. Then 2 + 3 = 5, and 3 + 5 = 8, giving us the whole pattern of 1 1 2 3 5 8. To get the next number, we add the previous 2 numbers, so we do 5 + 8 = 13, which is the correct answer.

Number series can also use subtraction:

$$10 \quad 8 \quad 6 \quad 4 \quad \underline{\quad\quad}$$

In this example what number are we always subtracting? The answer is - 2.

Number series can double:

$$1 \quad 2 \quad 4 \quad 8 \quad \underline{\quad\quad}$$

Each time the number doubles, which means it is added to itself. The next number would be 8 + 8 which means the answer is 16. If we did the next number after that it would be 16 + 16 = 32.

Sequences can divide:

$$40 \quad 20 \quad 10 \quad \underline{}$$

Each time the number is divided in half. To get half of a number, you have to figure out what number can be added to itself to get the answer. So are last number in this pattern is 10, what number can be added to itself to get 10? Think of it like this: ? + ? = 10? The answer is 5.

Number series can sometimes just be a pattern; there might not be any math at all:

$$1 \qquad 12 \qquad 123 \qquad \underline{}$$

There is no real addition going on here. The sequence just adds the next number in the number line to it. "To get the next number add another digit on the end. This digit will be one more than the last digit in the previous number." The next number would be 1234, then 12345, then 123456 …

Let's try some more tricks:

$$1 \quad 0 \quad 2 \quad 0 \quad 3 \quad 0 \quad \underline{}$$

The next number is 4. The alternating 0's are just noise to throw you off the trail. Our statement is "Add one to the last number that WASN'T a 0."

10   01   20   02   30   _____

"The next number will either be the next 10 in the series of 10's OR it will flip the tens and ones place." The last number was 30 so the next number will be 03. The next few will be 40, 04, 50, 05 ...

0001   0010   0100   _____

Binary anyone? "To get the next number move the 1 left by one place." The next number is 1000.

More Practice:

40   4   30   3   20   _____

6   6   5   5   4   _____

12   10   8   6   _____

40   35   30   25   20   _____

11   13   15   17   _____

3   6   9   12   15   _____

6   5   65   4   5   _____

7   6   7   6   7   _____

5   10   15   20   25   _____

8   6   4   2   _____

Answers:

40   4   30   3   20   2

6   6   5   5   4   4

12   10   8   6   4

40   35   30   25   20   15

11   13   15   17   19

3   6   9   12   15   18

6   5   65   4   5   45
(see we joined the 6 and the 5 to make 65? Now we join the 4 and 5 to make 45)

7   6   7   6   7   6

5   10   15   20   25   30

8   6   4   2   0

Appendix E: Number Equations Explained

This appendix tells you how to solve each of the equation building questions. This section can be the most challenging of all so we included a description how to solve each one.

1. 6 8 1 1 2 + + + / ()

In this question, the answer happens to almost already be in order. If you add 6, 8, 1, and 1, you get 16. Divide that by 2 and you get the answer, which is C. On most of these equations, you are just trying out different ways to solve the problem and seeing if you get an answer that exists.

2. 3 9 15 - x ()

The correct answer here is to multiply the first 2 numbers and then subtract the last one. That gives you 27 – 15 which is 12, or answer E.

3. 15 5 2 10 - - + ()

Add 15 and 10 to get 25. Then subtract 2 and 5. That will give you the correct answer of 18, or E. Don't pay too much attention to the parentheses in these questions, they don't make much of a difference most of the time in these questions.

4. 5 4 6 - x

Multiply the last two numbers, 4 x 6 = 24. Then subtract 5 and you have your answer 19, which is D.

5. 3 27 2 () / -

In this question you can be fairly certain you aren't going to divide by 27, so you should start by putting 27 on the far left of your imaginary equation. Divide 27 by 3 to get 9, and then subtract 2 to get your answer 7, which is A.

6. 2 5 1 2 / + x

Set up your equation like this: 2 + 5 x 1 / 2. This is a question that you do have to think a little bit about not having any parentheses. 5 times 1 is 5, divided by 2 gives you 2.5. Then add 2 for your answer 4.5 which is B.

7. 16 4 2 - / ()

Subtract 4 from 16 to get 12, then divide by 2. That gives you 6 which is answer E.

8. 9 3 -3 + x ()

Add 9 to -3 to get 6, and then multiply by 3 to get your answer of 18, which is C.

9. 1 2 2 3 + + x

Multiply 3 and 2 to get 6, and then add 2 and 1 to it to get 9, which is answer B.

10. 3 8 2 + /

Divide 8 by 2 to get 4, and then add 3 to get 7. That's answer E.

11. 6 3 2 + x

Multiply 3 and 2 to get 6, and then add 6 more for your answer 12, which is B.

12. 21 4 3 + / ()

Add 4 and 3 to get 7 and then divide 21 by 7 to get 3. The answer is A.

13. 2 2 3 5 x + + ()

Multiply 2 and 5 to get 10, then add 2 and 3 for a total of 15, which is answer A.

14. 4 6 3 2 () () / / +

Setup your equation like this: (4 / 2) + (6 / 3). Solving that equation gives you 2 + 2 = 4, which is answer B.

15. 24 2 1 x - ()

Multiply 24 and 2 to get 48, then subtract 1 for your answer 47. The answer is B.

Final thoughts: As we said before, this section is the most difficult for many. If these problems have given the student serious problems then we suggest making up some more practice problems to work with making various equations using the math operators. Make sure you have 1 more number than you have operators (1 1 + + for example will not make an equation!) Start simple and work your way up. What equations can you make with these sets?

2 2 +
2 2 3 + -
2 2 3 + - ()
2 2 3 4 + - x ()
2 2 3 4 5 + - x / ()

To further strengthen the skill in this exercise work with the order of operations and remember PEMDAS: Parentheses Exponents Multiplication Divide Add Subtract

Have you ever been sold on testing tips or seen testing tips as a part of the advertised education product to only see the tired list of "Be sure to eat a good breakfast!" and "Get a good night sleep!"? Well aside from quoting those worn out phrases we will not push this on you. We have actual words of wisdom to work out.

These are best served as conversation pieces or action items to be taken one or two in a sitting. Each page will have its own topic of discussion so feel free to skip around.

Appendix F: Critical Thinking, Testing Tips & Exercises

What is Critical Thinking?

Critical thinking is taking information into your brain, **processing the information** and using the processed information to make better decisions.

What does that mean to "process the information"? For our purposes in the test we are mostly talking about the logic that is happening when you try to solve a problem. When looking at three shapes and trying to determine how they are similar there is a logical **loop of questions** that plays out

"Are the shapes the same color?"
"Do the shapes have the same number of sides?"
"Do the shapes point the same way?"

Processing information can also come from the student's past experience, beliefs, or other reasoning skills.

When you want to train to win the test you have to think of how you are going to process information. Then given a question type what is your loop of questions?

The next pages go into more detail on these concepts.

Appendix F: Critical Thinking, Testing Tips & Exercises

The Loop of Questions and Training Habit

A morning routine may look like this: Wake up, brush your teeth, take a shower, get dressed, eat breakfast, leave the house.

This is a cycle of actions that is taken every day and very little actual thought must be taken since it is a habit. The same idea needs to be applied to the sections of the test. You see a question and you have a list of questions to help **process the information**.

Look at these number sequences:

5	10	15	20	25
10	11	12	13	14
8	6	4	2	0

Each of these shows a different pattern but the loop of questions is the same:

"Are we adding across the sequence?"
"Are we subtracting across the sequence?"
"Are we multiplying across the sequence?"
"Are we dividing across the sequence?"

Action: On an index card develop a set of questions for each question type in this book and practice using your loop of questions. Feel free to add questions to your card as you work through the problems.

Appendix F: Critical Thinking, Testing Tips & Exercises

You Tell Me! Creating Your Own Test

Nothing helps critical thinking like having the student create their own problems. Have the student use this drawing as a template to create logic problems like the visual sections in this book.

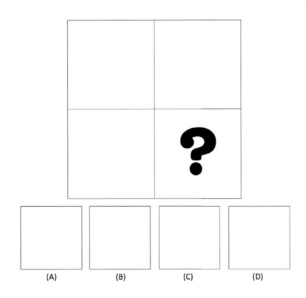

Action: Have the student create a set of problems for you to solve on scratch paper. The questions must be logical and they must be able to explain the correct answer and why the other answers are not correct.

Bonus: Have the student create other types of questions like number strings and number puzzles.

◆ + ◆ = ❓ | ◆ = 3

a) 5   b) 6   c) 7   d) 8   e) 9

Appendix F: Critical Thinking, Testing Tips & Exercises

Question Each Answer

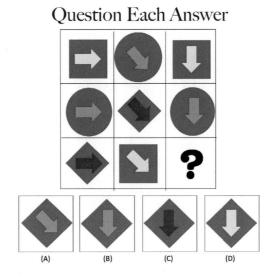

The test is asking you questions. Turn the tables and ask questions of the test! Here we want to find the right picture to fit the bottom right block. Let's have an imaginary conversation

You: "Answer A-D Why are you not the correct answer?"
Answer A: "I'm a blue diamond with a green arrow pointing diagonally. I am in the third column where all arrows point down. I am probably not the answer"
Answer B: "I have a green arrow that points down. I am pointing the right way but each row has the third arrow the same color as the first arrow. I should be red"
Answer C: "I am a red arrow pointing down, I may be the right answer"
Answer D: "I am a yellow arrow pointing down, I am not the right answer"

Action: Try questioning answers with a few practice problems in each section.

Test Each Answer

Similar to question each answer, we will now test each answer. This is a very powerful tool in acing any type of multiple choice algebra type test.

Look at this number series

$$4 \quad 5 \quad 45 \quad 6 \quad 7 \quad \_\_\_\_$$

A) 7   B)8   C)21   D) 4   E)67

This looks like a simple addition, add each number to the last. But what is that 45 in the middle of the string for? Well test each answer and see if it looks like it can fit mentally place each answer into the space and see if it looks right. Answer E is correct. Once placed in the answer spot you may "see the pattern" 4 and 5 become 45; 6 and 7 become 67!

Look at this Number Puzzle

a) 7   b) 6   c) 5   d) 8   e) 9

Substitute the Triangle for the 4 and require the problem as 4 + 3 on your scratch paper. Now we have 4 + 3 = ? Replace the answers presented to see which one fits the problem. 4 + 3 = 7? Yes, the answer is A.

Appendix F: Critical Thinking, Testing Tips & Exercises

Mental Gymnastics for Attention to Detail

In grade school you are given a sheet of math, it may have 5 or 10 of the same type of problem. Maybe you get 10 addition and 10 subtraction problems. You do the 10 addition problems, then do the 10 subtraction problems. Your ability to pay attention to detail is slightly dropped as you work through 10 of the same type of problem. You don't have to think "Oh this is an addition problem...what are the rules for addition?...ok time to do addition" You know all 10 are addition so you work them like an assembly line.

Action: Instead of working 10 of the same type of problem work one problem from each of the 9 sets in this book. The process of switching problem types after each problem forces you to examine the rule set.

"Ok it's a number series, in these the series could be addition, subtraction, multiplication or division."

"Ok it's picture categories I need to look for similar shapes, counts, colors, sides and so on."

Appendix F: Critical Thinking, Testing Tips & Exercises

Proverbs for Exercising Analysis Skills

Define Analysis: examination of something. Breaking complicated things into smaller parts to gain understanding.

Analysis is determining the intended meaning of some bit of information. When you analyze pictures for categories you are breaking the pictures into smaller parts to understand them. "Does each picture have a triangle?" is a good analysis question.

Here we will recognize your analysis skills by discussing proverbs. A proverb is a simple saying that has a deeper meaning. First break the proverb into parts, try to understand the parts and then guess at the overall meaning.

Have the student tell you what each of these proverbs means after their careful analysis.

"The early bird gets the worm."

"There is more to knowing than just being correct."

"A book holds a house of gold."

"A diamond with a flaw is worth more than a perfect pebble."

"Deep doubts, deep wisdom; small doubts, little wisdom."

"Dig the water well before you are thirsty."

Appendix F: Critical Thinking, Testing Tips & Exercises

Number Puzzles. This section is carried forward from earlier COGAT works. It is not a part of the COGAT 7 & 8 grade test but we include it here as a great exercise in critical thinking. Number puzzles ask you to abstract numbers into shapes and use them as number. It's kind of like a fore runner to Pre-Algebra and gets the student used to holding temporary variables in their mind while solving a problem.

1. 6 x ■ = (?) | ■ = 9

a) 46   b) 54   c) 63   d) 56   e) 52

2. 72 / △ = (?) | △ = 8

a) 9   b) 7   c) 11   d) 8   e) 6

3. ◆ x 6 = (?) | ◆ = 12 / 4

a) 15   b) 24   c) 12   d) 18   e) 24

4. 72 + ⬡⬡ = (?) | ⬡ = 7 + 2

a) 81   b) 90   c) 86   d) 76   e) 92

5. 37 - ✕ = (?) | ✕ = 7 x 2

a) 35   b) 51   c) 28   d) 30   e) 23

6. ■ + ■■ = (?) | ■ = 6 + 7

   a) 18   b) 21   c) 39   d) 37   e) 41

7. ■ + 7 = 9 + ■ - (?) | ■ = 14

   a) 0   b) 1   c) 7   d) 2   e) 3

8. ◆ - 4 = 17 - ◆ + (?) | ◆ = 11

   a) 1   b) 3   c) 0   d) 4   e) 2

9. ■ x 7 = (?) | ■■ = 12

   a) 26   b) 42   c) 35   d) 49   e) 32

10. ▲▲ + ▲▲ = (?) | ▲ = 3 x 7

   a) 46   b) 96   c) 84   d) 74   e) 78

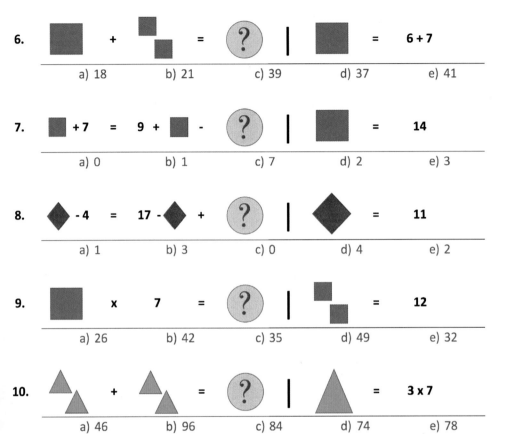

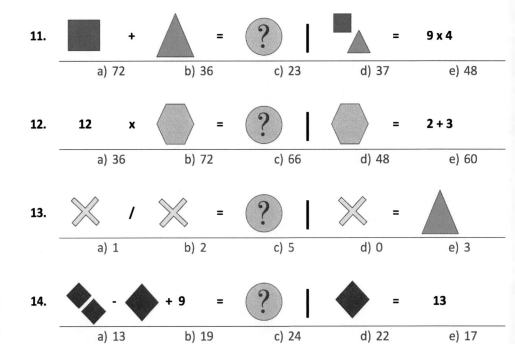

11. ■ + ▲ = ❓ | ■ ▲ = **9 x 4**

a) 72   b) 36   c) 23   d) 37   e) 48

12. **12** **x** ⬡ = ❓ | ⬡ = **2 + 3**

a) 36   b) 72   c) 66   d) 48   e) 60

13. ✕ **/** ✕ = ❓ | ✕ = ▲

a) 1   b) 2   c) 5   d) 0   e) 3

14. ◆◆ **-** ◆ **+ 9** = ❓ | ◆ = **13**

a) 13   b) 19   c) 24   d) 22   e) 17

15. ❓ **=** ⬡⬡ **+** ⬡ | ⬡ = **3 + 4 x 2**

a) 42   b) 33   c) 21   d) 24   e) 36

Number Puzzles: Answer Key

Question	Answer
1	B
2	A
3	D
4	B
5	E
6	C
7	D
8	A
9	B
10	C
11	B
12	E
13	A
14	C
15	B

This concludes our book. Be sure to check out our COGAT® Trainer apps on iTunes and Google Play. Just search for COGAT® Trainer and look for Polemics Applications.

Visit us at www.polemicsmath.com
Send all feedback to info@polemicsmath.com

Polemics Math